T0375190

Letting Go of Leo

HOW I BROKE UP
WITH PERFECTION

SIMI BOTIC

BALBOA.
PRESS

A DIVISION OF HAY HOUSE

Balboa Press books may be ordered through booksellers or by contacting:

Balboa Press
A Division of Hay House
1663 Liberty Drive
Bloomington, IN 47403
www.balboapress.com
1 (877) 407-4847

Because of the dynamic nature of the Internet, any web addresses or
links contained in this book may have changed since publication and
may no longer be valid. The views expressed in this work are solely those
of the author and do not necessarily reflect the views of the publisher,
and the publisher hereby disclaims any responsibility for them.

The author of this book does not dispense medical advice or prescribe the use
of any technique as a form of treatment for physical, emotional, or medical
problems without the advice of a physician, either directly or indirectly. The
intent of the author is only to offer information of a general nature to help
you in your quest for emotional and spiritual well-being. In the event you use
any of the information in this book for yourself, which is your constitutional
right, the author and the publisher assume no responsibility for your actions.

Print information available on the last page.

ISBN: 978-1-5043-9270-9 (sc)
ISBN: 978-1-5043-9271-6 (hc)
ISBN: 978-1-5043-9328-7 (e)

Library of Congress Control Number: 2017918079

Balboa Press rev. date: 12/13/2017

To my dad, mama, and sister Christiana, for making home a space
where it was safe to feel my feelings, safe to use my voice, and
safe to be myself. Thank you for teaching me to be strong, kind,
honest, and authentic. Thank you for helping me come home to
those values when I lost my way (many times). Thank you for
raising me to have faith – in God, in others, and in myself. And for
helping me believe in miracles. I love you, I love you, I love you.

Contents

BLISSFULLY UNCONCERNED / I'M GOING TO MARRY LEO

IN THE THICK OF IT / NOT WINNING AN OSCAR

THE LIGHT AT THE END OF THE TUNNEL /
THE ONE TIME I ATE A ROLL OF LAXATIVES

SHEDDING THE SHOULDS / TWO BANANAS,
REAL BACON, AND HAIRY ARMPITS

SHOWING UP / NAILING IT 23% OF THE TIME

Foreword by Katie Dalebout

Author, "Let It Out: A Journey Through Journaling"

The first time we spoke on the phone I knew I'd met a lifelong friend.

"You should come visit! Stay with us, we'll celebrate your birthday!"

We met online, but a few minutes into our first long phone conversation, Simi had already invited me (a stranger at the time) to stay with her in Columbus, Ohio.

It was the week before my 25th birthday and little did Simi know I was feeling completely lonely. Starved for community and actually pretty starved for nourishment since I'd been excessively dieting for years, I said "yes." The trip from my home state of Michigan to Columbus, Ohio was almost five hours. Not a super long road trip, but the longest I'd ever driven alone.

I didn't tell my mom I was going until the night before when I realized she'd see my travels on Instagram. I knew her reaction would be something along the lines of, "You're driving alone five hours to stay with your 'friend' you met online? Sim ... what? And her husband? Do you even know these people?" Her understandable trepidation made me feel even more anxious as I packed up my overnight bag, downloaded hours of audiobooks, and picked up snacks.

When I arrived, Simi and her dogs met me in the backyard and every ounce of hesitation dissipated instantly. Simi was magnetic, inviting, warm, and made me laugh instantly. She made me feel so cozy that I told her everything about my life, from the breakup I was still hung up on to my deep lingering issues with food and my body. Simi not only listened but truly heard me, made me feel seen, related to me, and gave me the non-judgemental advice I needed.

That weekend ended up being profound for me in a couple of ways. Not only did I spark a new friendship with Simi, but simply by spending time with her I gained clarity on how I wanted my life to unfold. I admired the relationships, career, community, and home she'd built for herself. Above all, I deeply admired the nourishing relationship she modeled with food, movement, her body, and herself. At the time I was struggling to find my footing in all of the above.

That weekend I ate, drank, and laughed more than I had in a long time. For the first time I wasn't obsessing about what or how much I was eating. I simply followed Simi's intuitive lead and enjoyed food. I have no idea if she knows how profound that weekend was in healing my relationship with food and myself, but I'll never forget what a turning point it was for me.

They say you become the sum of the people you surround yourself with. I wanted to be near Simi, her friends, and her family, so I escaped my life in Michigan and made the journey to Columbus as often as I could. I even plotted moving there so I could insert myself into Simi's life, where I knew I'd be included.

Ultimately, I realized this would be cutting the line. Simi created the life she'd dreamed of with trial and error, time, and experience (which you'll read all about in this book). It took her years to curate her community, cozy home, meritorious marriage, and most importantly the relationship with herself that I admire most. I gave up my dream of simply inserting myself into Simi's life and instead worked on creating an admirable life of my own.

Ever since that first weekend meeting Simi, she has become one of the most significant people in my life. Beyond being a powerful example for me, she's the most supportive friend I have. A good friend braids your hair. A great friend flies across the country pregnant to be at your book launch.

When my book was released, Simi launched into help mode even though she was super pregnant and stricken with terrible nausea. It didn't stop her from flying to New York City with extreme flight delays to stay in a tiny hotel room with me the night my book came out. During my launch party in a crowded organic cafe in the West Village, she stood up on a table and announced that I had something to say because she knew I'd be too shy to do it myself (and regret it if I didn't).

This is just one example of what you're dealing with when it comes to the level of kindness and empathy in the author of this book that you're about to read. In the years we've been friends, she's supported me, loved me, and talked to me for hours about everything from ex-boyfriends to new boyfriends to hating my body to learning to love my body. She's listened, let me cry, and made me laugh ... whatever I needed.

I'm not telling you this to brag about our friendship, but so you truly get who she is. The type of person everyone wants to be around. And when you're around her, you want to snuggle up to her and gush because she's incredibly empathetic, present, relatable, and funny (oh, and has the best laugh in the universe).

The good news is you'll get to experience all of her in the pages of this book (except her laugh, which can often be heard in her Instagram stories). Reading this book, I felt the same coziness I feel when I'm actually around Simi. This book is the inside of her brain poured out onto the pages. Simi's experience coaching and mentoring, commitment to self-awareness and growth, creativity, and willingness to be vulnerable are what make this book exceptional.

I'm not just saying this because she's my best friend, I truly loved reading it. Meanwhile, it took me forever to start writing this foreword. Not because I didn't want to (I was honored she asked me), but because I didn't want to let her down ...I wanted it to be perfect.

Then I read Simi's intro, which you're about to read, too. It took me off the hook. It reminded me that I didn't have to make something perfect for this person I love and admire so much. I just needed to make something real because that's the thing Simi has taught me most in our years of friendship: Real is better than perfect.

So, congratulations on buying this book. I'm so happy to get to share my best friend with you.

-- Katie Dalebout

Author, "Let It Out: A Journey Through Journaling"

A Note on Writing This Book and the Lesson I Had to Learn (Again)

Writing this book brought up things I wasn't expecting.

I had planned to write a book about breaking free from the prison of perfectionism. I was going to share 10 lessons that taught me to stop freaking the eff out about everything from food to body image to career to love to ... yeah, basically everything. I had worked through so much of my personal crap that I (naively) expected this book to just flow out of me.

I was going to write a perfect book. A perfect book about no longer needing to be perfect. The irony of this was lost on me.

For months, every time I sat down at my laptop, I was met with paralysis. I couldn't write.

For months, I watched the blinking little line on the gigantic blank page with terror. It taunted me!

For months, I didn't know words. I didn't know thoughts. I didn't know anything!

At first I blamed my lack of progress on the sheer size of the project. *Oh, it must be that this book is so big that it's overwhelming me.*

Then I blamed it on having my son, Alyosha. *Before Osh, I could write anytime I wanted to! I could sit down when the mood was right and then all the perfect words would just come right out. Now, I can only sit down at certain times and they just aren't good times to write, I guess.*

But plenty of people write books and plenty of people have babies. And, eventually, I got annoyed with my own excuses.

I sat down with myself to get to the bottom of it.

What's really going on here, Simi?

I was freaking the eff out. I was scared out of my mind. Scared that the book wouldn't be perfect.

The voice inside yelled, *WRITE IT PERFECTLY! WRITE SOMETHING AMAZING! MAKE OPRAH PROUD!*

I mean, give a girl one publishing package and it goes straight to her Oprah-loving mind.

When I tried to write that perfect book, I couldn't. And the blank pages reminded me that there are no such things as perfect books. Or perfect words. Or perfect lessons. Or perfect people (other than Oprah).

I re-learned that perfectionism is its own form of torture that makes even life's most awesome experiences feel like failures.

I had already learned this lesson about food and my body and travel and true love and pregnancy and labor and motherhood and friendship and curly hair. I guess I just needed to learn it about book writing, too.

So, rather than fail at writing something perfect, I decided to write something real.

I used to freak out all the time about food and my body and not being in control and not being good enough. I freak out a lot less now. And that's what this book is really about.

It's about my stories. Messy stories about what I've felt and experienced and learned. Stories about how I've hurt and cried and laughed and messed up and grown and healed. Stories about eating an entire jar of peanut butter without choking to death. Stories about my inner thighs rubbing together. Stories about having a baby and actually liking it. Stories about becoming an attorney and actually *not* liking it. Stories about being brave enough to try something new. Stories about mistaking laxatives for candy. Stories about learning to show up for the good stuff *and* the hard stuff and, perhaps most importantly, learning to show up for myself.

BLISSFULLY UNCONCERNED / I'M GOING TO MARRY LEO

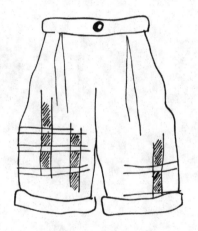

I Think I'll Ride Bikes Instead

There were bowls of candy all over my childhood house.

In any room where people gathered, you better believe my mom had a beautiful crystal bowl full of mini chocolates. As a kid, we were never told how many pieces we were allowed to have. The chocolate was always available, and as far as we knew, we had permission to eat the treats anytime we wanted.

I can remember occasionally unwrapping a mini Reese's Peanut Butter Cup and eating it. There were other candy options, like Hershey's Kisses and dark chocolate squares, but I've never been one to pick anything else when chocolate-wrapped peanut butter is an option.

For every time I ate a piece of candy, I can remember even more times when I played next to the bowl of candy and didn't even think about it. There wasn't much to think about really, since it was always there. I could have one, or more, whenever.

My mom always cooked dinner for our family. Sit-down meals with green salads and grilled meats and fresh bread. No matter what happened during the day, we always sat down together as a family. It was a time where we never answered the phone, no matter how many times it rang. "The answering machine can get it!" my mom would declare. And we'd go back to fighting over who'd be first to

3

dip a piece of bread in the *moca* (a Serbian word for the juice left behind from grilled steaks). *Moca* was a real delicacy in our house.

Once in a while, my mom would make dessert. But when she didn't, we were always welcome to help ourselves to the ice cream sandwiches in the freezer and the candy scattered around the house. We weren't told to finish everything on our plate. We weren't told sugar was bad. We weren't told we had to earn a treat. Honestly, food was just food. I don't ever remember thinking it was a big deal or feeling conflicted at all as a kid. My mom loved to cook and she loved to share what she made with us. I loved enjoying everything she prepared.

Our house was often the place where other kids came to hang out. We would have pool parties and sleepovers because my mom loved to host. I had a few friends who would come over and, every single time, comment on the bowls of candy and easy access to sugary treats in the garage freezer.

"I can't believe you have so much fun food at your house! My mom never lets me eat sugar! She says it's addictive and will rot my teeth!"

I'd touch my teeth to make sure they weren't rotting out of my mouth. Nope, we were good. I couldn't help but wonder, *Did they not brush teeth at their house? Maybe that was the problem.*

They would hover around the crystal bowls, eyeing the candy. Walking toward the bowl. Then walking away. Then walking back. After a few back-and-forths, they would start eating. Not one or two pieces, but handful after handful, piece after piece. It seemed like they couldn't unwrap them quickly enough, and sometimes I worried they might accidentally eat some of the wrappers. Once finished, they would hide the empty wrappers in the sofa cushions, pleading, "Don't tell your mom I ate that many pieces, OK?"

I was so confused because they acted like my mom was going to be upset about candy. *Why would she put candy out if we weren't allowed to eat it?* I wondered. I tried to explain to them, "My mom doesn't care how much candy you eat," but they still didn't want her to know. So I let them shove candy wrappers in our furniture and watched them eat so much candy that, when dinner time came, they had no room in their bellies for *moca*.

I thought to myself, *I guess when someone tells you that you can't eat candy, then you have to eat a lot of it every chance you get.*

I felt sad for them because candy is yummy but eating a lot of it really fast usually means you get a tummyache. Also, because my mom's cooking was awesome and now their bellies were so full of candy that they didn't have room for her homemade meatballs or her special red sauce.

When they would head home the next day, I'd watch my mom go from room to room collecting the crumpled foils tucked deep behind the cushions while she smiled at me with that mom smile that means, *I love you a lot a lot a lot.*

"Want a piece, sweetheart?" she'd ask as she re-filled the candy bowls.

"Eh, not really," I said. "I think I'll ride bikes instead."

If only that relationship to Reese's Peanut Butter Cups had lasted.

Chaffing Wool Shorts

I was six. Or eight. I'm not sure exactly. I pick a different age every time I tell this story.

My sister, Christiana, recently asked if I remembered helping our mom pull weeds as kids. I didn't. Not because it happened and I have a horrific memory for chores, but because my attention to detail was so poor that my mom wouldn't let me anywhere near her garden. As if that was some kind of punishment. JOKE'S ON HER.

Anyway. I can't tell you my exact age but what I know for sure is that I was a kid. Maybe six, maybe eight, definitely not seven. I was a kid who had to wear a uniform to school. And this uniform involved shorts. Plaid, wool shorts.

After a day of running around on the playground and also probably learning some math (like I said, I can't tell you exactly what we did that day because my memory is not 100%), I came home from school.

The insides of my thighs were tingling and burning.

I went straight to my room to take off my school clothes and get into comfies. My husband, Tim, says he's never seen anyone get into pajamas when they get home more quickly than I do. He doesn't say it as a compliment, but that's how I take it. This is clearly a skill I've been mastering since childhood.

I dropped my shorts to the floor and noticed something between my thighs. I had big red welts and a few smaller, chafed spots that were bleeding.

"Fffffffff!" I sucked air through my lips and between tightly gritted teeth as I tried to assess the damage.

"Mom!! Look at this! My thighs are bleeding. They hurt so badly!"

She met me at the bottom of the stairs to take a peek.

"I'm sorry sweetie. I bet that does hurt! Let me get you something to help."

My mom grabbed a towel from the drawer and ran it under icy cold kitchen sink water. Every move my mom made was done with intention and care. As you might have guessed, she's very detail-oriented. Once she was finished soaking and chilling every fiber of the towel, she led the way to the family room.

She held the dripping cloth in one hand and fluffed the couch pillow with the other, helping me get nice and comfortable. I laid down and she positioned the cloth between my thighs.

"How does that feel?" she asked.

"So good. Thanks, mom."

It really did feel so good. Why more people don't just lay with wet towels between their thighs is a mystery to me.

7

The next day at school, I was ready to rock 'n' roll (*Thanks, mom!*). I wore a bandage full of Neosporin on each of my inner thighs. I did NOT wear those awful wool shorts.

On the playground, a bunch of friends and I started an animated game of "Cats." Unsurprisingly, this game involved us pretending to be cats. We designated a spot on the playground as the spot where we ate our imaginary food. Another spot was our imaginary litter box. The rest of the playground equipment was the "furniture" that we'd climb all over. Because that's what cats do.

As we pounced around in our very footloose and fancy-free, cat-like fashion, I noticed one of my friends was wearing her wool shorts. I was honestly worried about the wellbeing of her inner thighs.

"Those shorts rubbed the inside of my thighs and made them hurt so bad! Do they do that to you?" I asked.

She looked at me a little confused and said, "Uh, no. My thighs don't rub together. But my legs are smaller than your legs."

For the first time in my life, it occurred to me that people were different sizes. I looked at her legs. Then I looked down at mine. She was right. Her thighs were smaller than mine.

"Oh," I said. I couldn't explain why, but I felt embarrassed. "I wish my thighs were smaller like yours so they didn't have to bleed when I wear shorts."

"Yeah," she replied. "MEOW!!!"

With that, we went back to being cats for the rest of recess.

It would be a long time before I ever felt comfortable wearing shorts again.

Semi Butt Itch

When I was in fifth grade, we moved to a new town.

I was very into movies (still am) and totally thought I was going to marry Leo (more on this later, don't worry). Based on what I had watched, I understood that this move could really be my moment to shine. I might discover I was secretly an awesome soccer player (I would not discover this), become a cheerleader (I did not become this), start a babysitter's club (negative here), or fall in love with my soul mate (nope). This move meant I got to go to a new school where I didn't have to wear a uniform, and we all know how well wearing a uniform went for me. It also meant that I got to go to a school where there were boys. From all the movies I had watched, I knew this meant I would probably be doing a lot of kissing.

As I prepared for my first day of school, I was nervous. I was going to ride a bus for the first time, and I thought there was a high probability I might kiss a boy on that very bus ride. I needed to pick out the perfect outfit because I would need to remember the outfit I wore when I got my first kiss on my first bus ride to my first co-ed school. Oh, the pressure.

I went with a matching khaki vest and skort. For anyone born after 1990, a skort is a pair of shorts with a flap of fabric that tricks people into believing you're wearing a skirt. It fooled nobody.

Nailed it.

My mom snapped a few obligatory first day photos of us on the driveway and then it was time for me to catch my ride. The big yellow bus pulled up (*Just like in the movies!*) and I boarded. I looked up and down the rows, trying to decide where to sit. Per the movies, I knew the back of the bus was where cool kids sat, but I didn't want to seem too eager. I also knew I got car sick and looking out the front window helped, but I didn't want to look too loser-ish. Five minutes in this new world and already so many choices. Suddenly, I missed my uniform.

I walked right to the middle of the bus, where there were a few empty rows, and sat down alone. Since this was before cell phones, I had nothing to look at to help me seem "busy." Instead, I stared at the seat in front of me, running my pointer finger over the very vein-like lines on the very fake-looking leather. The original Instagram.

As I made figure eights with my hand, my mind wandered and I began to dream about my first kiss. I'm not sure how long I was fantasizing about a kiss by my locker, but before I knew it a group of boys came and sat down next to me.

HOLY GUACAMOLE IT'S HAPPENING! WHICH ONE WILL I KISS?! I wondered.

These three boys looked eerily like Hanson, with their long hair, beanie hats, and baggy jeans.

WAS I REALLY GOING TO GET MY FIRST KISS FROM A GUY WHO COULD BASICALLY BE IN A BOY BAND?!

"Hi, I'm Simi."

"Huh? Cindy?" one replied.

"No… SIM EEEEEE. SIM EEEEEE BOAT ITCH" I said.

"Wait, your name is Semi Butt Itch?!" another replied. And they all laughed.

"Good name for you, since you're fat and ugly," the last one chimed in.

My chest felt tight and my stomach dropped to the floor as I realized today probably wasn't the day for my first kiss. I adjusted my skort, trying to pull it down over my "fat and ugly" thighs, looking out the window and doing my best to believe that, *I am rubber, you are glue. What you say bounces off me and sticks to you.*

A few minutes later, the boys got bored with me and laughing at each other's bad jokes. Finally, they left me alone.

I hated them for being so mean. But I hated myself even more for being so "fat and ugly." For giving them a reason to be mean to me. Even though I hated them, I really wanted them to like me.

If I had said the right thing or looked the right way, they would've been nicer. Maybe I would have gotten my first boyfriend, like in the movies, rather than a terrible nickname that would follow me around for year. No, not maybe. I was *sure* of it.

If I were different, they would see me differently and treat me differently.

It was all my fault.

If I felt rejected by someone, no matter how hurtful that person was acting, I wanted that person to like me. Because being rejected made me feel like I had done something wrong. Like something was wrong with me.

I didn't want to be Semi Butt Itch! I didn't want boys on the bus to think I was "fat and ugly."

If I could make them un-reject me, then I would know I was OK.

I wanted to be OK. I needed to find a way to be OK.

It's the Puppet Lady

When I was a senior in high school, I signed up for AP Psychology. On the first day of class, our teacher walked in with spiky blonde hair and quirky glasses, and I couldn't shake the feeling that I knew her.

I turned to my friend and asked, "Does she look super familiar to you?" Nope, not to her.

Maybe I've seen her walking in the hallways? I tried to reason with myself. But as the weeks rolled by, I just *knew* that I knew her! I couldn't place it, but I was confident that it was more than a casual hallway nod-and-smile.

Right around week four, she was telling us a story about how powerful puppet play could be in child psychology. She went on to share that she had been the child psychologist at the school for many years, and filled her office full of fun puppets to help children open up and give voice to their feelings.

THE PUPPET LADY!

I was filled with a brief moment of excitement as I connected the dots. *I knew that I knew her and now I finally know from where!* She was the puppet lady! When I was a kid, I loved playing puppets with the puppet lady. Every year around the holidays, I would ask

13

my mom to take me shopping so I could buy her a fun new puppet to give her as a gift.

It took me a few moments to connect the other dots, which were that I saw a child psychologist, and wasn't just miraculously getting out of classes to go play with puppets. I almost spit water across the room from laughing. I excused myself from class to go have a proper laugh in the bathroom. My mom and I had a good laugh later that night, too. Nothing like finding out your best gal with the puppets was actually your psychiatrist all these years later.

As a kid, I had a lot of anxiety and spent a majority of my days worrying. I worried about having friends. I worried about being left out. I was scared to act or talk or look differently than the people in my class, because I thought it would make me less likeable and more rejectable.

These daily anxieties went beyond wanting to fit in. I was constantly afraid something bad was going to happen to someone I loved. This was back in the day of pagers, and I had a special code I would send to my mom's pager in case of an emergency: 411. I would text her 411 anytime I needed to get in touch with her (which was an emergency in my mind).

At the end of school, I watched the clock like a hawk. I knew the exact time my mom was supposed to pick me up from our after-hours program, and if she was even 30 seconds late, I would start paging her from the lobby phone. If she was a few minutes late, she might get five or six pages. If she was 15 minutes late, we're talking closer to 50. It's not that I thought she had forgotten about me, I was just terrified she had been hurt in some kind of horrific accident.

I have zero internal questions about why little Simi went to see the puppet lady from time to time. I also have zero questions about why grown-up Simi sees the grown-up version of the puppet lady from time to time: So that my loved ones don't have to get 50 text messages and a smoke signal when they get caught at a red light on their way home.

IN THE THICK OF IT / NOT WINNING AN OSCAR

Ross and Rachel Are Meant to Be Together

I grew up with parents who talked openly with me about God and their Christian faith. It never felt like they were forcing their beliefs on me. More like they were sharing wonderful things they'd learned. We said prayers at night, hung icons in our house, and attended church. It was something we shared and something that I believe brought us close. I can't remember a time when I wondered, "Does God really exist?" God's presence was something I understood as fact, the same way I knew any other fact.

The earth is round: fact.

Night happens after day: fact.

Ross and Rachel are meant to be together: fact.

While some things in life made perfect sense to me — like God, or Ross and Rachel ending up together — other things didn't come as easily. Like college. Well, more specifically, why everyone seemed to love going to college so much. That was something I really didn't understand.

Woof. That freshman year was a tough one for me. Kudos to colleges for offering a few free counseling sessions to each student. You know I took advantage of that!

I would spend my entire session crying to the counselor about how I didn't have my life together. I'm not sure how much he and I actually accomplished during our time, but I got my money's worth of tissues.

I was really struggling. I missed my family. I missed hugs. I missed feeling like I still had time to figure out what I was going to do with my life. When I got to college, there was no more time! *NOW IS THE TIME!* Or at least that's what a very fired-up senior enthusiastically yelled at us on our welcome tour around campus.

His words came back to haunt me every time I changed my major. Which, if you're wondering, was quite often. I leaned into the Bible and the buffet to help me cope. I spent the majority of my time doing two things: 1) Attending events put on by a Christian organization for college students and, 2) Eating as much food as I could fit into my belly. My freshman year at college is when I first started to really binge.

After a worship service or Bible study, I would stop at one of the dining halls on my way back to the dorm. I would eat as much as I could there: egg sandwiches, smoothies, stir-fry, icing-filled cookie sandwiches. When I was done, I would buy an after-meal snack at the little dining hall grocery store. My favorite was a jumbo-sized bag of lime-flavored tortilla chips and queso, all of which I would eat in one sitting back in my dorm room bed while I watched a movie. I would eat and eat and eat until my stomach felt so full that it might rip open. Then and only then would I be able to stop.

After a semester of bingeing multiple times a day, almost every single day, I gained weight. In fact, when I went home for winter break,

I was wearing exclusively pajama pants, as nothing else would fit. Even though none of my clothes fit me, I was too distracted by my own emotional discomfort to realize that my body had changed. That is, until we took Christmas card photos and I saw myself. I did not feel good about what I saw. When I saw the images I made the connection: *Oh my gosh! The reason why none of my clothes fit isn't because of some weird college laundry situation … I've gained weight!*

I freaked out. I told my mom she couldn't use the photos because I felt awful about myself. She hugged me. She told me I was beautiful. She reminded me that weight fluctuations were normal. She took me to buy some non-pajama pants that fit.

But, even in pants that fit, I couldn't stop thinking icky thoughts about my body.

Suddenly I realized that I had gone for months without even one guy being interested in me. I had listened to stories of other people going out on dates, getting invited to frat parties, and being hit on by guys in their Astronomy 101 class.

I had no dates!

I went to no frat parties!

I was not getting hit on!

I couldn't even escape my feelings of inadequacy at Bible study! At the Christian community events, conversations regularly turned to dating and marriage. People would talk about having the "DTR" conversation, which I learned meant to "define the relationship." People were pairing off to DTR and plan their futures together! Meanwhile, I was wearing pajama pants to class and eating pints of Cold Stone Creamery's Birthday Cake Remix in the dark.

NOW IS THE TIME AND I AM FALLING BEHIND!

This only made me want to eat another frozen burrito the size of my head.

But, I went back to school after that winter break on a mission. A mission to be the kind of girl that a guy would want to DTR with — or at least who got invited to a frickin' frat party. I also wanted to do these things in something other than pajama pants.

So I started to run.

A few of my college friends were into running, so I asked them if I could join. These girls were so nice. Even though they were much faster and more experienced, they were willing to run with me from the very beginning. It was less like running and more like fast walking with a lot of breaks. They never complained or left me behind once. Even though the running made my lungs burn and my legs feel full of heavy liquid, I *did* like getting out of the stuffy dorm and doing something, anything, that had nothing to do with school. In other words: anything that wouldn't remind me how much I didn't have my life figured out.

A few months later, I ran my first half marathon. Technically it was more of a shuffle/walk, but I finished and that made me feel very accomplished. Until that day, I had never thought of myself as a runner. Each year in highschool, there was always that day when we had to run a mile in gym class. It gave me serious anxiety and I was always last to finish. When I ran track growing up, it was really more me tripping and falling over the hurdles, praying nobody noticed. I thought people were straight up lying when they said they were craving a run. The half marathon made me feel like I could surprise myself. Like I could do things I never knew were possible!

I was hooked.

After that first half marathon, I started to subscribe to running magazines. It's not official until you get a subscription, right?

I would read every word of every article on how to make me a better runner. I started to add in interval runs and cross training days and hill workouts. Every month, the magazine would come and every month I would add any and all of the runner tricks to my regime. Including the tips about food.

Each magazine arrived with more insight on nutrition that promised to maximize my performance and help me lose weight. And I tried to do it all. Maybe I didn't know what I wanted to major in or do for the rest of my life, but at least I could feel in control of this.

I trained for one race after another and, after two years, decided it was time to graduate to full marathons. I would wake up early, hungover, to run. I would skip class to run. I would go for runs late at night to shake out the day.

On top of the runner's high, I also noticed that I could put my jeans back on. Soon, those jeans were too big. So I bought new ones.

I was straight-up addicted to running. There was literally nothing that could get in the way of my run. On holidays, on weekends, on vacations … I never missed a run. I trained for races in Cancun in 100-degree weather; on bear-occupied trails in northern Wisconsin; and through the crowded streets of Istanbul. I was terrified to miss a run. I didn't want to know what would happen to my body if I did.

I stopped going to Bible study because I was too busy working out. *I don't need those things anymore*, I thought. *All I need is another run.* Church was optional. Working out was not.

Divine Intervention via Double Stuffed Oreos

Four years later, I was still running religiously.

I left law school and headed home to visit my parents for winter break with a print-out of my running schedule. I never went anywhere without it. I also had the recipes for the food that I was "allowed" to eat so that I could stay "on track." When they saw me, my family shared that they were worried about my weight loss but I brushed off their concerns. It wasn't that I knew I had issues and was trying to deflect. I honestly thought they didn't get it.

Can't they see how healthy I'm being? Why are they acting worried? This is what healthy looks like!

My family told me they wanted to go to church that Christmas morning, and I was slightly annoyed because it would cut into my running time. I'd have to wake up extra early. And so I did. I layered on my winter gear before heading out into the frigid and dark early morning air. With each mile my body relaxed a little more until I finally arrived home with a sense of relief that, at least for Christmas day, my run was done.

When we got to church, a blanket of panic covered my body. *Communion.* I didn't know how many calories were in that bite of bread. I didn't know what ingredients they used to bake it. I didn't have a snack scheduled at this time. Communion didn't fit into any of my rules and I couldn't find a way to relax enough to take it. I wanted to scream or cry. Instead, I made up some story about a stomachache so I could go to the bathroom and miss it altogether.

Once there, alone in the stall, I prayed.

Freedom.
Freedom.
Freedom.

The prayer surprised me. The words felt like they were coming from a deep place I hadn't listened to in a while. To be honest, I hadn't prayed in a long time. Not because I didn't believe in God anymore, but because I had forgotten I needed Him. I was busy worshipping other things. And considering I was locked in a bathroom stall terrified to eat a bite of bread the size of a quarter, that was clearly not going well.

I prayed some more.

Help me break free.

Please, God.

Suddenly my behaviors didn't feel so healthy anymore.

Please help, I prayed.

I waited until I was sure communion had ended, and went back into church. I spent the rest of the day with my family, celebrating Christmas by eating the food I had prepared, careful not to go over the recommended serving size for each dish. At the end of the day, I reviewed all of my calories and was able to go to sleep without too much anxiety since I had stayed within my daily limit. Oh and don't worry. I remembered to set my alarm to get up and run the next morning.

I went back to school a few days later knowing that there was something off about how I was treating myself. But I was also too terrified to disrupt the structure I had built. Mentally, I wasn't ready to change. But physically, something inside my body was. Now, many years later, I can see the physical shift that was about to happen was an answered prayer. At the time, it felt like living a horrifying nightmare.

I started to gain weight. I wasn't eating more or exercising less, but the scale started to creep up. I was beside myself! I added in more miles, more 90-minute boiling hot yoga classes, more leafy greens, and less of everything else. I ordered books on how to self-hypnotize myself to weigh less. I made vision boards filled with the skinniest images I could find. I juice cleansed and bought weird pills at the grocery store that claimed they would clear my liver. I did it all. Binges followed.

I was eating the smallest amount of food I had ever eaten in my entire life and exercising more than ever before. But the number on the scale kept rising. So I reached out to a nutritionist and made an appointment with my doctor.

They both asked me, "Have you tried eating [a very restricted number] of calories a day?"

Ummm ... Yes.

"Have you tried completely giving up sugar?"

Ummm ... I haven't eaten sugar in over a year.

"Have you tried going paleo or vegan or [insert other trend]?"

YES AND ALL AT ONCE, TOO!

They were stumped.

They both, independently, recommended I continue to do what I was already doing, and threw in a few extra rules for me to follow, assuring me that the weight gain was probably a plateau that I could push through. Nobody once suggested my behavior was restrictive, concerning, or dangerous. They told me that I was "doing everything right" and to "just keep going!"

But I kept going like that for years and nothing changed. No matter how hard I tried, I couldn't lose any more weight. My body was clinging to every pound she could. I was beside myself and had run out of ideas. That's when I stumbled upon Geneen Roth's book, "Women, Food and God." I devoured every page, reading it twice in one week. I didn't want to put it down. It changed my life.

In the book, Geneen says, "Replacing hunger for divine connection with Double Stuffed Oreos is like giving a glass of sand to a person dying of thirst. It creates more thirst, more panic."

Yep. I had been drinking sand when I really needed water. I had been starving and rationing and running, trying to make my way to love. I was thirstier (and hungrier) than ever.

That next week, I took a note from the book. Rather than make all of my decisions from a place of fear that something was wrong with me, I tried to trust: "Trust the longing, trust the love that can be translated into action without the threat of punishment. Trust that you will not destroy what matters most."

That Sunday morning, I decided to do what felt like love. I didn't run. Instead, I lay in bed and cried. I was scared to stay home, but felt like it was what I needed. So, I stayed. I trusted. And when I somehow survived a morning in bed, I decided to go to church.

Since Sunday mornings had been reserved for my long runs, I hadn't been to a service in as long as I could remember. But that Sunday, I got out of bed, put on a dress, and headed to church.

When I put that communion bread on my tongue, I cried for the second time that day. I closed my eyes. I prayed.

Thank you, God.

For that moment, I felt loved. I felt OK. I felt free.

I Bet Beyoncé Doesn't
Eat Stale Cookies

It was 7:12 AM and I needed to be at the court by 8 AM. (To clarify: I was a summer associate in law school at the time, not playing professional women's basketball.) I tried on my third suit for the day and, like the two before, this one was also squeezing across the front of my thighs. It felt too tight and I wanted to scream.

I didn't remember my suits fitting this way the last time I had to wear one. Panic set it.

I finally decided on a black dress. *Black is slimming, right?* I reasoned.

My skin itched and squirmed as the silk inner lining rubbed against my unshaved legs. I pulled on a blazer and felt the sleeves squeeze my upper arms.

Hours later, finally alone in my office after hours of talking about who would reply to who on what date, I closed the door. I was sweaty in a way that can only be facilitated by a too-tight suit jacket in a highly air-conditioned building. Cold hands, clammy armpits. I needed a break from being me. I opened up the internet and started scrolling for a mini escape.

I spent a lot of time obsessing over celebrity magazines, gobbling up the latest gossip, closely examining movie stars' bodies, and daydreaming about how good my life would be if I could just look and live like them. It was like the grown-up version of a fairy tale.

Anybody who knows me will tell you that I used to know all the pop news. Every. Single. Thing. There was no baby name, no divorce detail, and no movie star workout plan that I couldn't tell you about. Losing myself in the photos and stories about celebrities was a way for me to escape the unhappiness, discomfort, and discontent I felt in my own body and my own life. For the 10 minutes I spent checking in on the newest love connections and who was headed to rehab, I got to live in a fantasy that felt better than my real life.

Celebrities all seemed happy, loved, and content. Even if something bad happened, their lives somehow still appeared magical! I wanted to feel magical in my life, especially when bad things happened.

I fantasized about having a thin Hollywood body.

I'd think about how if I could just be super skinny like an actress, cut-off jean shorts would hang off my hips while I danced at a music festival, flower crown tilted just so. In that body, I could float around a pool on a swan raft and look photo-ready from every angle. In that body, I would never have to go to court with sweaty armpits and a skin rash caused by too-tight business attire.

I'd do anything to escape from being me. Scrolling, searching, praying for some secret formula to turn my life into some fun, light-hearted movie trailer. I thought that if I could just "detox" my body down to celebrity standards, then I would finally be able to really LOVE my life.

Have I mentioned that I have zero acting skills? Unless you count the one time I was a moderator in the "Vagina Monologues" in college. Yes, the moderator. I was given that role because I wasn't even a good enough actor to give voice to my own vagina.

MY OWN VAGINA.

So, there I was, a woman who couldn't even finish the sentence, "If my vagina could talk," trying to detox her way to winning an Oscar and a life she could love.

If a celebrity was quoted saying she did a specific juice cleanse, you can bet your bottom dollar that I was on that company's website ordering their $500 juice cleanse two minutes later. If an actress said she did HIIT circuits, ballet class, or boot camps to get role-ready, you know what I was up to the next day at 6 AM! And when my favorite singer said she ate a certain number of calories to lose weight, I was busting out my excel spreadsheet and counting my little heart out for weeks to come. I would spend hours and hours and hours searching the internet about specific celebrity plans and trying to piece together bizzare internet stories about what stars "actually ate."

I juiced. I fasted. I counted. I macro-ed. I jumped. I ran. I stretched. I sweat. I tonic-ed. I potioned. I saged. I went vegan. I went Paleo. I tried my hand at macrobiotics. I drank that ridiculous skinny tea that did nothing but give me diarrhea.

If a celebrity did it, I did, too. Even if "doing it" meant crapping my brains out. I was willing to crap my brains out to look like those women in the magazines. That's commitment.

There was so much frantic hope in this process. Opening up my computer or buying the newest magazine to discover the latest celebrity secrets was like a shot of adrenaline to my brain. I would almost get euphoric imagining how much better my life might be if this secret was the one that actually worked.

The cycle was predictable at best, obsessive at worst: I'd feel discouraged about the way I looked in a photo someone tagged me in on Facebook, a work skirt that fit too tightly, or something else uncomfortable. I would think about how celebrities always looked perfect in photos, wore sample sizes, had super fun jobs, and always seemed to be smiling. I would turn to Hollywood to escape my own discomfort — and try to find a solution.

TELL ME WHAT I SHOULD DO! TRANSFORM ME FROM THIS TROLL THAT I AM! I would beg.

I had convinced myself that if I followed these (probably fake) plans perfectly, I could come out on the other side victorious. I would swell with hope at this idea. And then I would crash a few days later into a box of stale cookies dunked in peanut butter and tears.

Get it together, Simi! I bet Beyoncé doesn't eat stale cookies!

This cycle went on for years: I would feel uncomfortable, then try to escape via pop news and celebrity plans, then dive face first into stale cookies, then feel even worse about myself than before. It didn't occur to me that there might be something wrong with the cycle. I simply believed there was something wrong with me.

Try harder, cleanse cleaner, eat less, spin more, I told myself.

So I kept scrolling. Looking for answers. Looking for motivation. Looking for the secret.

Not only did I actually try "The Secret" (from what I read, this was all the rage with celebrities), I tried just about everything else. At one point, I read that connecting with my primal pleasure and animal instincts would boost my metabolism. So I got onto all fours and pretended to be a wild animal. I growled and rawr-ed. It did not make me lose weight. Or make me happy. It did result in rug burn and some understandable confusion for my neighbors.

I needed someone to blame for the times when I felt rejected, left out, and not good enough. So I blamed myself. I blamed my body. Because blaming my body meant I was just one diet away from being fixed.

Swallow Them Whole
Like a Candyconda

When one of us is in a particularly abrasive mood, Tim and I like to call the other out for being a "snapdragon." It's our way of bringing gentle humor to a very not gentle situation. It feels more loving than "Stop being an a-hole, mmmk?" and gives the person who's being a snappy a-hole permission to say "I'm sorry" and talk about what's really going on without needing to get defensive.

We can all be snapdragons sometimes. But I used to be one a lot of the time.

I've had a lot of moments where I've snapped at family members. And bless them for putting up with me and loving me through them all. I'm not sure if it's just me, but I have always felt like I was safer to be a little more of an a-hole with my family. Because, for better or worse, they are stuck with me and have to love me no matter what. At least that's what I tell myself. Sorry mom!

When I was at the deepest and darkest part of my relationship with food — and therefore the deepest and darkest relationship with myself — I did something I had never done before and have never done since. I snapped at someone who I'm not related to. I snapped at someone who did not have to love me no matter what. I snapped at my best friend.

Red flag that things were bad bad bad bad.

In Chicago, Tim and I had a candy tree. This metal wall hanging was intended for votive candles, but we filled the little glass cups with seasonal M&M's instead. At the time, M&M's (or any sugar at all) were absolutely not on the list of foods I allowed myself to eat. In classic "I have eating issues" fashion, I would encourage other people to eat the sugary treats that I never let myself enjoy. It was very normal for friends to come to our apartment and eat our candy. *That is why we had it out! So people could enjoy it!* It would be weird to put candy out and then tell your guests, "No, that's not for you." Clearly it was for them.

It had been a long week, thanks to my 5 AM runs, 6 PM 90-minute hot yoga classes, and studying for law school finals.

I was terrified that exams wouldn't go well, so I had shifted into Ultra Control Mode in an effort to ward off any less-than-desirable outcomes. This meant exercising longer, eating as clean as possible (code for restricting even more than usual), and telling myself that I just needed to lose a few more pounds by the end of finals. I didn't want to eat anything "bad" or miss checking a single box on my to-do list. I couldn't afford to fail!

I distinctly remember feeling especially exhausted on that week's Friday morning run. Not only physically, but in every sense of the word. It was still dark out and as I ran through the blackness I thought, *It wouldn't be the worst thing in the world if a car didn't see me and just accidentally hit me. Then, at least, I could stop trying so hard and lay down to rest.* It didn't happen, so I had to find the energy to run all the way home. And study. And do hot yoga.

I was trying to function off green tea, carrot sticks, and adrenaline. Considering my fantasies involved being hit by a fast-moving vehicle,

I'm going to go out on a limb and say this approach wasn't going well.

That night, my BFF came over. As you can probably guess, it was the highlight of my week. We plopped down on the couch to watch a 90s thriller, our favorite genre. We'd been watching 90s thrillers together since the actual 90s, when we'd go to Blockbuster to rent gems like "Sleeping With the Enemy" on Friday night.

As the movie started, she reached for a few M&M's.

I was so hungry I just wanted to be able to eat an entire bowl of M&M's. An entire swimming pool of them! To swallow them whole like a candyconda. To crack the shells between my tongue and roof of my mouth before letting the chocolate melt down my throat. To never stop eating them. The yellow ones first, because they're my favorite. Then blue. Then green. Then red. *HELL! I would even eat the brown ones!*

But I couldn't. I was out of calories for the day and those candies had sugar and dyes and fun in them. All things that were off limits for me.

Watching her eat that first M&M was more than I could take (*It was YELLOW! IS THIS SOME KIND OF SICK TORTURE?*).

My heart started to race. I hated myself so much. The self-loathing was so strong that it filled my chest and lit every one of my hair follicles on fire. The top of my head burned with so much heat that I started sweating.

I wanted to SCREAM!

I wanted to scream it all.

I'll never be able to sleep through my early morning run!
I'll never be able to have fun at happy hour!
I'll never be able to have fun on vacation!
I'll never be able to have fun at brunch!
I'll never be able to have fun at a wedding!
I'll never be able to have fun!
I'll never be able to wear shorts!
I'll never be able to rest on a weekend!
I'll never be able to bake cookies and not binge!
I'll never be able to stop sucking in my stomach!
I'll never be able to say the right thing!
I'll never be happy enough!
I'll never be likable enough!
I'll never be good enough!
I'll never be smart enough!
I'll never be skinny enough!
I'll never be enough!

I'LL NEVER BE ABLE TO EAT SOME FRICKIN' M&M'S WHILE WE WATCH A TERRIBLY BAD BUT YET SO GOOD MOVIE!

AHHHHHHHHHHH!

She was chewing an M&M when she looked up and saw my face. I can only imagine what it looked like. I was basically one M&M from throwing myself on the floor.

"Sim? Is it OK that I just had an M&M?"

With so much hatred for myself and so much envy for her casual M&M eating, I replied in a cutting tone, "I don't know. They're Tim's M&M's. He might want them. You really should have asked him first."

TIM'S M&M'S?!

First, they were not Tim's M&M's. He didn't own the apartment's candy. Second, they were literally there for anyone and everyone to eat.

As soon as the nasty words came out of my mouth, I wanted to cry. Making someone who I loved so much feel so badly did not make me feel any better. It made me feel way worse.

She put the other M&M's back into the little glass holder.

"I'm so sorry. I am sure Tim won't mind if you eat those M&M's," I assured her, trying to cover up my nastiness by continuing the lie.

LET IT GO SIMI! TELL HER EVERYTHING! TELL HER WHAT'S REALLY GOING ON!

But I didn't.

"It's OK, Sim."

I could tell she was hurt and it was hard to believe that it was OK, that she actually forgave me. Not because she lies. She doesn't lie. *I'm the one who lies about M&M's!* It was hard to believe that she really forgave me because I spent so much time telling myself I had to be perfect to be loved. It seemed too good to be true that I could be so not perfect and that she would love me anyway.

So, I sat there waiting for her to change her mind about the whole forgiveness thing. To tell me I was a horrible, selfish liar. To never watch another movie or eat another M&M on my couch again.

But she stayed.

Now I know I don't have to be perfect to be loved. I know that my friends and my family will love me, stay with me, and forgive me through the hard moments. And every time they do, they teach me a little more about how to love myself, stay with myself, and forgive myself.

Now, almost a decade later, we still watch 90s thrillers every time we're together. Only, today, I let myself eat the M&M'S *with* her.

I'll Just Run These Two Miles

There were three occasions when I thought Tim was going to propose to me during the summer of 2010. He did not propose on any of them.

With each rejection, I grew more and more worried that he didn't love me the way that I loved him. (This was my experience, not his. He thought we were just having innocent picnics in the park.) I thought I wasn't good enough. That he had changed his mind about our future. After all, what other explanation could there be? Certainly not that the ring had been delayed three times. Certainly not.

I started to do the thing I do when I feel insecure: I began to overanalyze. I would hang on every word he said, obsessing over the tone in which he said it. I scanned his facial expressions and body language for any hint that my worst fear was about to come true. And, as I was investigating his every move, I noticed that he was definitely acting strange.

THERE I HAVE IT! The proof I needed. While I was patiently (ha) waiting for a proposal, he was secretly plotting our breakup.

A few different times, I asked Tim if everything was OK. "You seem a little weird." (My tactic to make it about him, not me.)

He assured me that everything was OK and he didn't feel weird.

CLASSIC PRE-BREAKUP ASSURANCE. He couldn't fool me.

I just knew it in my bones: I wasn't good enough. I decided I would try to lose more weight. Maybe that would help.

At this time in my life, I was running a minimum of seven days a week. If there had been 12 days in a week, I would have run 12 times. I had a very strict schedule for running and refused to let myself skimp on any of the workouts. If the plan said three miles, I ran three miles. If the plan said 20, I ran 20. When I was in a boot for three months thanks to a stress fracture, I went to the gym everyday and did that many miles on the elliptical. Never a step less.

So I woke up one Saturday morning like I did every Saturday morning: ready to run. I laced up my shoes and headed for the door.

"Hey, wait!" Tim called. "I want to come with you!"

OK. So of course I loved to have company on my runs. And of course I loved to spend time with Tim. But his classic move was to come on runs with me and then insist that we walk. I think I've already made it clear that this was just not an option for me. The thought of having him with me, trying to make me walk, made me anxious.

But I obliged.

"OK, I have a four-miler today. Are you up for four?" I asked.

"Sure, yeah, whatever! I'll be ready in a minute." His laissez-faire attitude about the distance made me even more anxious. I could tell he wasn't taking this as seriously as I was.

As we started the run, Tim seemed even weirder than he had been the weeks before. Every question I asked him was met with a one-word response. He claimed it was because he's "not good at talking" on runs. But I felt like it was something else. He seemed like he needed space. So, naturally, I probed more. I was determined to find out what was going on!

One mile into the run, right in front of Chicago's Adler Planetarium, he came to a halt.

"Sim, my ankle is really hurting. I need to walk."

I KNEW IT! I KNEW HE WOULD WANT TO WALK! I thought, feeling vindicated.

After the vindication came the terror. *I can't walk. I have to run a full four miles. This is the only time today I can squeeze this run in, since we are visiting his parents later today. One mile is nowhere near enough! What will happen to my body if I only run one mile? I don't want to be a failure! I don't want to fall behind. I really need these miles so I don't self-destruct.*

"Tim, you know I have four miles today. I can't stop now! I told you this before we left."

Terror shifted to frustration. *He insists on coming on my run, acts super weird, and now is trying to make me walk.*

"OK, but it's no big deal! Let's just walk the next three together. Or sit with me for a second?"

"SIT?! You know I have to get my run in or bad things happen!"

"Bad things?" he asked, so confused.

"I don't have time for this, Tim. You sit here; I'll just run these two miles, turn around, and meet you back here. By then, I'm sure you'll feel good enough to run the last mile with me." And, before he could say anything, I was off.

As I ran, I felt my chest tightness release. I was going to get the miles in. I didn't have to be scared anymore. I relaxed and ran as fast as I could. *Everything is going to be OK.*

At the time, I didn't think I had done anything wrong. I thought I was strong and committed and driven. I was focused and fueled by willpower. Other people might stop to walk with a loved one, but I didn't have time for that. I had to earn relaxing walks with loved ones, and I could only earn those walks after my "real workout" for the day was done. I thought I was doing something right because nothing could keep me from checking it off my to-do list. My rules and schedules, including those daily workouts, were the only way to know that I was going to be OK.

Fifteen minutes later, I circled back to find Tim sitting on the Planetarium steps. He looked a little sad. I ran up, bouncing from my left foot to my right, inviting him to "Come on! Let's finish the last mile strong, together!" He did not look like he was interested in finishing the last mile strong.

He put his head in his hands and took a deep breath.

When he looked up, he locked his eyes with mine. "Sim, can you just sit down for a second? I have something I want to say."

Every inch of my skin stood up. Still running in place, hysterical alarms sounded in my brain: *IT'S HAPPENING! HE'S BREAKING UP WITH ME. DO SOMETHING, DO SOMETHING, DO SOMETHING!!!*

"I'm not sitting down. Anything you need to say to me, you can say to me while I'm standing up," I said. *THERE! TAKE THAT! You might be dumping me, but I'm going to stay standing, so at least I can quickly run away after it happens!*

I was really showing him the mature, loving, amazing woman he was letting go.

He shook his head, took another deep breath, and proceeded.

"OK Sim. Whatever you say. At least come closer so I can hold your hand, will you?"

Weird that he wants to hold my hand when he dumps me, but I do really love holding his hand. I walked toward him, awkwardly leaning forward as he sat on the huge cement steps and I stood in silent protest. I gave him my hand.

One last handhold.

"OK. So, you know how you've been feeling like we aren't on the same page and I've been acting weird?"

BRACE FOR IMPACT. HERE IT COMES.

"Uh huh …"

"Well, it's because I've been keeping something from you. Well, planning something for you."

"Huh?"

The words from here were all a blur.

Out of the little pocket in his shorts he took a ring box. He opened up the box, revealing a perfect yellow diamond ring. I was shaking and my ears were ringing. I didn't hear a thing he said. He probably said something along the lines of, "You can be really selfish and too obsessed with exercise but I still love you, so will you marry me?" Or at least that's what I would have said to someone who left me to go run two more miles when I was trying to propose.

Regardless of the words, I knew he wasn't breaking up with me and I knew that I got to spend the rest of my life with the most incredible person in the world. We sat on the steps hugging and shaking and laughing. Pure joy!

For a few minutes, I even forgot about that last mile I was going to run.

~~Slightly~~ Very Embarrassing, But True

Rewind to 2005. The jungle juice was flowing, the tank tops were bejeweled, jeans were embossed, and Kelly Clarkson's "Since U Been Gone" was blaring on the speaker.

It was 3 AM. Up until childbirth, this was the only time I was ever awake at this hour. I was at a friend's birthday party and a cake fight broke out. Yes, you read that right. I don't know who started these sugary shenanigans, but I was ready to go home. When I turned around to walk out of the door, some rude person who didn't understand how badly I needed to be asleep smashed cake into my face. That's when I looked up and saw Tim.

I felt like there was a magnet in my chest that was pulling me toward him. I had to be close to him. But, you know, that feels creepy when you don't actually know the person's name. So I just licked icing off of his finger (*WHAT?!*). He said, "You're hot." Then we parted ways.

If you know us now, you're likely really struggling to imagine this interaction. I promise it's true. I am ~~slightly~~ very embarrassed I licked cake off a stranger's finger, but I will not edit out my embarrassing behavior. That's how committed to honesty I am here.

Until next time, hot cake man, I thought as I stumbled back to my dorm room.

Again, ~~slightly~~ very embarrassed here.

I call my mom almost every morning. I like to think she loves this about me, but I haven't actually asked her. So, like clockwork, I promptly called my mom the next day to tell her, "I met the guy I'm going to marry last night."

How would I make this happen? I had a few ideas ...

During college, I worked at the most delicious bagel shop (shout out to Bagel & Deli). I did not know that I had Celiac disease at the time and ate approximately two to three bagels a day. The beauty of bagels is that they work for every meal. Breakfast? Throw an egg on there. Lunch? Add a veggie. Dinner? PIZZA BAGEL! Dessert? Tuck a chocolate chip cookie right in the center. If eating exclusively gluten could give you Celiac disease (it can't), then this is where I would have developed it.

At this time, Tim would regularly come in and order the "Messy Katie." Every time I made him this sandwich (five times a week? Gosh, he ate a lot of bagels), I would draw a heart with the honey mustard and think, *please ask me out please ask me out please ask me out* before wrapping the foil around his lunch.

Friends ... THIS WORKED.

A little less than a year later (hey, I said it worked, not that it worked quickly), he asked me out on Valentine's Day ... WITH A BAGEL DECORATED LIKE A VALENTINE'S DAY CARD.

Be still my bagel-loving heart.

Coincidence? I think not! More like the power of intention. Or damn good bagels. Or licking icing off his hand. Whatever. Something worked!

Well, sort of. I was so nervous to go on a date with him that I had to leave work early because I couldn't stop throwing up. Not a good situation when you work in food service. I ultimately had to cancel our date due to a "stomach bug" (read: crazy nerves). Then my roommates proceeded to record a video of me crying, "I'll never get another chance!" in heart-covered pajama pants.

I did get another chance. A few nights later we went out for Tim's birthday. It was my first time meeting a lot of his friends and I made a great impression. As we were sitting around his apartment chatting, I literally fell off a stool and knocked my head against the tile floor (not drunk, just that impressive). I could tell they were all jealous Tim got to date me.

Still slightly very embarrassed here.

The next few months were a blur of fun. We went out. We danced. We ate midnight grub. We made out. We BBQ'd with our friends. We drove two hours to try good Indian food. We partied. We rode bikes. We made out some more. We stayed up late talking. We woke up early to talk some more. We listened to the "Scrubs" soundtrack on repeat.

I savored every second of it.

For the first time in as long as I could remember, I didn't worry about my body or obsess over what I ate. It didn't even occur to me to restrict, think about the calories in that late-night slice of pizza, or binge. I just had fun. I felt so full. When I looked at pictures, my smile was huge. I had no idea how my body looked because I was smiling so big that I couldn't see anything else. I was too busy living my life to worry how I *looked* living it.

Soon, I graduated from college and moved to Chicago to start law school. The fears of rejection and failure and not being good enough, or special enough, or the best, all crept back in. I did my best to control and smooth them away. But my fears got heavier. My neuroses grew more intense. My fun got way less fun. I kept trying to make myself smaller until every problem would just disappear. It didn't work.

THE LIGHT AT THE END OF THE TUNNEL / THE ONE TIME I ATE A ROLL OF LAXATIVES

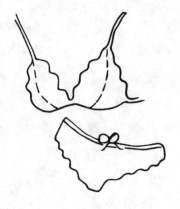

The Dirty F Word

Toward the end of my first year in law school, I had a brief due in my legal writing class. "Brief" is a fancy law school word for "paper" that makes the assignment seem much scarier than your average paper and plays to the egos of future attorneys.

Ohhhh, you write papers in your grad school? Interesting, in law school we write BRIEFS.

Anyway, this one was regarding whether a parrot could be considered a service animal. Exciting stuff, right? The thrill of it all was almost too much to handle. Especially when you use words like "brief" and "regarding"!

I spent a lot of time on this brief because legal writing was a serious struggle for me during my first semester of 1L year. A partner I worked for once told me, "Well, Simi, we know writing is not your strength." To overcompensate for my apparent writing weakness, I spent all second semester making up for my first semester shortcomings. With every reasoning and analysis I delivered, I just wanted my professor to think I had done a good job.

At the beginning of Friday's legal writing class, we all turned in our briefs, and I was feeling good about mine. This is a red flag in the practice of law: Anytime you feel good about something, someone is about to burst your bubble. There were all these super specific rules about the exact time the paper had to be turned in and other formatting requirements to teach us how to follow rules when we turned things into the real courts one day. If you didn't follow all the rules perfectly, your paper would be bounced, which means you instantly lose 20% and had one hour to fix it. Well, I wasn't worried because I am a Rule Follower (capital "R," capital "F," because the English language requires we capitalize names).

I was wrong. Apparently, I hadn't checked my paper a final time and the page numbers on the last few pages didn't print because the printer ink was running low in the library. At the end of class, my professor called me to the front of the room to announce my paper was getting bounced. I wish I were exaggerating when I say that I lost my damn mind.

I quickly grabbed the paper and ran into the bathroom where I proceeded to wretch my body onto the cold, hard floor. The loudest, most insane noises you've ever heard were flying out of my mouth. I don't know you or the noises you've heard, and I can still make this statement with 99.9% certainty. I was hyperventilating. It was as if all the stress and all the little failures from the entire first year in law school — heck, my entire life — had built up to that exact moment. I called Tim on my cell phone and he actually thought someone had died.

I told him, "*I'M* DYING!!!!" I mean, did he not understand the importance of my BRIEF?! This was not a regular paper!

I couldn't stop crying but had to get my paper corrected ASAP. I went to the library where I continued to cry as I reprinted my assignment. Two very kind and very concerned librarians came over to ask if I was OK. When they confirmed that I was, in fact, *not* going to die, they kindly asked me to quiet down, please. Once I had my paper properly printed, I headed to my writing professor's office to turn it back in. The whole walk to his office I prayed that I'd stop crying. And, of course, for an A.

Lucky for me, I just happened to be wearing a white peasant top that day. For those wondering, yes, I did and do continue to wear peasant tops even though they went out of style in 1998. I like to pretend that my life is an episode of "Dawson's Creek."

How do I remember what I was wearing, you might ask?

Well, because I cried all the tears that day and they were so abundant that they actually dripped down my face, neck, and chest, soaking through my top. So, there I was in a completely see-through white top, with a face that looked like I had gone a few rounds with Floyd Mayweather, entering my professor's office.

Professionalism at its finest, no doubt. *WHO IS WONDERING HOW I DIDN'T LAST IN THE LEGAL PROFESSION?!*

I tapped lightly on his door and he told me to come in. When he saw me, sheer terror crossed his face. A ticking time bomb had entered his office.

WHAT?! HAVE YOU NEVER SEEN A GIRL CRYING DURING A WET T-SHIRT CONTEST BEFORE?!

Clearly, he had never been to spring break in Cancun.

I handed him my paper. He told me he knew how hard I had been working to improve my writing skills. He was honestly a great teacher.

Bless his heart, he tried to tell me that, "Everything is going to be OK," and it was "just one paper."

"I don't want to FAIL!" I choked out.

All I could think about was how I wanted to get out of there before the frog in my throat jumped out and smacked him in the face. I was about to exit the room when he said "Wait, I know what will make you feel better." He handed me a smattering of stale Tootsie Rolls from a bowl on his desk. He did not offer me an A.

"Thanks," I lied, wishing it had been a handful of mini Reese's Peanut Butter Cups because everyone (except my sister) knows Reese's are superior to Tootsie Rolls. I left the room, smashing the chocolate stumps in my warm fist.

I headed back to the bathroom, closed the stall door, and ate the nasty Tootsie Rolls while I cried some more. My brain was so squished. It was so full of everything I wasn't doing well enough. All the ways I wasn't enough. All of my failures and the things I needed to do to repent for them. There was so much in there that I couldn't think clearly. Yet all I could do was think. All of my swarming thoughts and self-criticisms and fears were suffocating my brain. There was no space left. No space to breathe, to think, to be. I could feel myself crumbling under all the pressure.

Something about that bathroom stall (or was it the mass hysteria and crap load of stale candy lodged in my molars?) reminded me of a therapy session I had when I was in college. I'd scheduled a session after a similar breakdown, that time triggered by an unwelcome C in a geology class that was lovingly referred to by my classmates as "Rocks For Jocks."

WHAT?! I was FAILING a class that was supposed to give A's to people who never went to class because they were too busy throwing balls around?!

Anything less than an A was failing to me. I also know nothing about sports.

I remember the therapist telling me:

1. Getting a C wasn't the same thing as failing. It actually meant average. He told me this as if it would make me feel *BETTER* about it.
2. Failure could be viewed in a different way than how I was currently seeing it (which was as follows: the world was crumbling down around me, nobody would ever love me ever again, and my life was essentially over, so please serve strong coffee at my funeral because I can't stand when you go somewhere and they serve that watered down stuff).

He kindly explained to me that failure, or a C, could actually be seen as an opportunity to reflect, learn, and pivot.

OK sir, I remember thinking. *That sounds nice and maybe failure means that for you because you live in this woo-woo world of therapy but I don't have a choice! I need to be perfect! It's who I am.*

And you know what else? He always served me watered down coffee when I would arrive for our sessions. So maybe he should have used that as an experience to reflect, learn, and pivot toward stronger coffee.

He told me I needed to stop making the F word (failure) so dirty.

"Why do you feel the need to be perfect?" he asked me.

"So that I can get a good job."

"Plenty of people get great jobs with C's on their transcripts," he told me. "Now, why do you *really* care?"

"So that I can make people proud. You know, that way they know I am good enough."

"There we go!" he said, as if I'd just told him something he knew all along. *SO WHY DID YOU ASK THEN, SIR?* "And when you say 'good enough,' good enough for what?"

I had a feeling he already knew the answer to this one, too. But it seemed rude not to respond, and I really didn't want him to think I was rude.

"Good enough to make people want to love me."

He nodded. I could tell he definitely knew that answer already, too.

I'd left his office and headed to Starbucks to get some stronger coffee, apologizing for taking up space on the sidewalk to every person I passed along the way. On that walk I wondered, *What if failure could feel different? What if I could feel different?*

Four years later in that law school bathroom stall, time had passed but not much had changed. A C still sounded like failure. I still felt like I had to be perfect. And I was still wondering if I could ever experience it all differently.

Those Aren't Candy

During my 1L year, I had serious digestive issues. I was constantly nauseous and chronically bloated. We lived within walking distance to a Target and I think I took 200 pregnancy tests that year. Probably not what the government intends you to do with your student loan money.

That summer, I finally saw a doctor who took my complaints seriously. She tested me for a host of autoimmune diseases and discovered I have Celiac disease. She told me there was no cure, but that I needed to cut gluten out of my diet, and stop using any gluten products that came in contact with my body.

Gluten, huh?

I had no idea that gluten was even a thing. I left the office feeling relieved that there actually was an issue that we identified, but also overwhelmed because apparently gluten was in pizza and beer and my favorite Aveda shampoo. *UGH, the essentials.* This was before everyone and her mother was "gluten free," so the nurse at the front desk filled my arms with packets to read, and gifted me a small bag of gluten-free cookies to enjoy. They were awful and I did not enjoy them. But you better believe I ate every last one of them while I cried thinking about all the delicious cookies I would never get to eat again.

Simi Botic

Once I was done being bummed out about it and could finally wrap my head around the day-to-day realities of Celiac disease, I really started to fear food. I was scared to go out to restaurants because something might have been cross-contaminated. I was scared to eat at friends' houses because they might think I was high-maintenance. I started to be less and less social and more and more controlling with food.

Once we started back for our 2L year, my food issues reached an all-time crazy.

A competitive environment paired with the Celiac diagnosis operated like a magnet that drew out all of my regimented intensity, obsessive scheduling, and perfectionism.

I became obsessed with "clean eating," which meant that I didn't let myself eat anything I felt could harm my body. I spent all of my down time reading about everything that I shouldn't eat. Different philosophies had different rules, so I decided the safest bet was to skip out on everything that any plan said I shouldn't eat. At one point I was restricting calories and about 90% of all food.

I packed perfectly measured lunches and snacks every day. My social life consisted of tea dates and hot yoga classes with friends so that I never had to eat something prepared by anybody's hands but my own or, *God forbid*, drink a beverage with alcohol. I regularly excused myself from plans because, "I don't think I can get anything without gluten there," or, "I've just got too much school work to do, sorry!" After two workouts a day, eating the bare minimum, a full school load, and a job, the only thing I had energy to do in the evenings was binge watch episodes of the remake of "90210." My brain didn't even have the capacity for quality television, and that's not an exaggeration.

I snapped at loved ones. My mind was so obsessed with food ingredients and counting calories that I struggled to give someone else my attention in even the most basic conversation. My energy was low, my libido was lower, and my period non-existent.

But most weeks when I got on the scale, the number was moving down. And people kept saying that I looked, "so amazing!" So while everything inside me screamed *Wrong!!,* I decided I must be doing something right.

Did I mention I was very hungry?

Spring break rolled around and a group of my friends planned a trip to Puerto Rico. My life had turned into one exhausting, monotonous cycle and I was so excited for a vacation. But I was on the brink of a breakdown thinking about how I would keep up my strict eating and exercise routines at the beach. I committed to getting up early each morning for an extra long workout, treading water in the ocean to burn extra calories, and drinking as little booze as humanly possible for the week.

HOW FUN DO I SOUND?!

I don't know if it was the heat or just being surrounded by people who weren't starving themselves, but my hunger was on a whole new level. I could hear a constant and audible growl coming from my stomach.

On our third day there, we were lounging on the beach. I was ravenous and didn't know what to do! I had already eaten my handful of raw almonds and had no other food on me. I started to scavenge through my friend's beach bag. I found a small white container full of round candy tabs.

THANK YOU, LORD! I prayed. With each one I would say *OK, Sim, last one*. But these chalky, multi-colored tabs were the most decadent thing I had consumed that year and I couldn't stop myself. Twenty tabs later, my friend emerged from the ocean.

"I am so sorry but I just ate all your candies. I was so hungry! I promise I'll pay you back or buy you more at the store near our place later today."

"Candies?" she asked, looking confused.

"Yea, whatever those fruity tabs were. I ate them all."

"Uhhh … come here for a sec." she said, leading me away from the group.

I walked over to her, slightly distracted by a cramping sensation in my stomach.

"Sim, those aren't candy," she whispered, leaning in close.

"Huh?" I asked, the cramping getting more intense.

"Those are my fiber pills to help me go to the bathroom when I travel …"

CRAP.

Eating French Fries and
Not Hating Myself

I will never forget when I got to my lowest adult weight. It was the day before I left for a moot court competition in New York City. That competition was one of my most treasured law school experiences, yet I remember feeling distracted by food the whole time. I was worried about what I would eat. If I would be able to count calories. If I would have the energy to perform well. If I would be able to get all my workouts in.

We got second place at that competition and I wonder now if the outcome would have been different if I'd been able to give it my full brain power and my full attention. This is the thing about a body struggle (or really any struggle, I imagine): It takes all of you. It is all-encompassing. And when you *do* come out of it, only then do you realize what you missed.

Every now and again I have a moment like this, where I realize what I sacrificed to the perfection gods. And it makes me sad. I take those moments to humble myself enough to say "I'm so sorry" to my past self for everything I kept her from doing and "I'm so sorry" to my present self for all the memories I don't get to have today. Then I give myself the gift of forgiveness.

I spent that entire trip swimming in my clothes. My pinstripe suits from J.Crew. My jeans. Even my running tights were getting loose. I remember thinking, *Wow! This is what it feels like to be small!* And then I panicked because I didn't want to lose it.

I had barely eaten in weeks, was running every morning before the competition, and was pumped full of adrenaline. So, after the final night of the competition, when our team went out in the city to sing karaoke and celebrate our hard work, it didn't take me long to feel the vodka sodas. After a few, I was, as my dear friend calls it, "hammer drunk." I was smashing French fries into my face, ordering shots of tequila, and belting out Britney Spears at the top of my lungs. The only time I could really eat or let loose was when I was pumped full of alcohol, which happened close to never.

I woke up the next morning feeling like death. Someone might as well have been banging an actual hammer inside my head. My morning run (because, yes, I did get up to go) was really a series of mini trashcan-to-trashcan sprints, where I threw up vodka and tequila and French fries and shame. I made myself do that for 30 minutes before I headed back to the hotel to shower.

I went out to breakfast that morning and felt so hungry I couldn't even stand it. I ordered pancakes and bacon. I ate them all. And when I threw them up later because I was so hungover, it was followed by more of an insatiable appetite. I was hungry.

I cried on the flight home from New York. I didn't want to leave the city where, for at least a few hours, I had let myself have fun. I didn't want to go back to the routine and the rigidity and the classes and the pressure.

When my moot court partner asked me why I was crying, I told him, "I just really love New York."

What I meant was that I just really loved eating French fries and not hating myself for a few hours. But that seemed weird to say out loud.

When we got home, something shifted. The scale wouldn't go down anymore. It started to go up. And I would never again see that number I saw the day before I left for NYC, no matter how hard I tried. It was an unnatural and unhealthy weight for my body, and what I've learned over time is that my body's healthiest size will NEVER require me to do unhealthy things to live there.

When I started to gain weight and feel like I was losing control over my ability to shrink my body, I was BEYOND TERRIFIED. I thought watching that number rise on the scale each week was the worst thing that could happen to me. There are a lot of awful things happening in the world, a lot of serious tragedy, and in my mind gaining weight was worse than all of it. That's embarrassing to admit, but it's true. The terror of gaining weight — which felt the same as being rejected by the world, strangers, and every person I loved — was suffocating. I couldn't breathe and you know what happens when you can't breathe? You panic! I panicked.

I did everything I could to get more air, to breathe.

I thought I was being punished for not having enough willpower or not being disciplined enough. I thought it was evidence of what every fitness magazine and diet book had been telling me for years: that my body couldn't be trusted and needed to be micro-managed.

But the "willpower," the discipline, the micro-managing: It didn't work this time. Nothing that had worked in the past worked anymore. It felt like the part of my brain that had fueled my previous intensity was burning up. My attempts to restrict were met with a simple "nope."

Nope.
Nope.
Nope.

It was a simple nope, but it was strong.

Our culture is so diet-centric that I had come to believe that weight loss and being on a diet or "cleanse" were the ways to experience true health. I had confused the word health with the word skinny. And when I was at the most intense and restrictive moment in my relationship with food, I had actual health professionals encouraging me to restrict more. I'm shaking my head thinking about the number of times I dropped hundreds of dollars on cleanses, potions, and superfoods to rid the "unhealthy" from my body. I wanted to be ~~healthy~~ skinny so badly!

If I had continued to lose weight while punishing my body with restricted food and over-exercising, I wonder if I would've ever changed my behavior. I was so programed to believe that weighing less was a good thing. I thought that the less I weighed, the healthier I would become. The smaller I was, the more I would be loved. My restrictive eating and ridiculous exercise behaviors had some seriously negative side-effects, like feeling isolated, losing my period, and sobbing hysterically in a coffee shop when I ordered a soy latte and they accidentally put cow's milk in there instead (Lord. Help. That. Barista.). But, at the time, they were sacrifices I was willing to make, challenges I was willing to overlook, to continue seeing a smaller number on the scale.

The weight gain felt like a painful crack in the perfect wall I had been building around myself for so long. Back then, I hated cracks because they made me feel imperfect. But, as Leonard Cohen says, "There is a crack in everything. That's how the light gets in."

The light started to creep in (and the number on the scale started to creep up), and it illuminated things I couldn't see before. I was able to see how unhealthy my behavior was and what true health could look like.

When I first discovered intuitive eating, it felt so scary to me. It felt so counter-cultural to listen to my body. But, over time, I learned to define things in different, more empowering ways. It was only once the light — my weight gain — got in that I was able to really ask myself, *What does a healthy life actually look like to me?*

Does health look like what I had been experiencing? Does it look like:

- Ignoring my body's hunger signals in favor of eating at a time and in a quantity determined by someone who has no idea about my special condition, needs, or what it feels like to live in my body?
- Skipping out on human connection in favor of ensuring that I can count everything in my food?
- Eating in a way that is unsustainable in the long term, triggers my body's survival mechanisms, and causes me to binge eat?
- Determining how I'm allowed to feel about myself and what I'm allowed to do in my life based on my most recent food choice or the number on the scale?
- Living with an all-or-nothing mentality?
- Letting the number on the scale be the main indicator of my health?
- Exercising for calorie or fat burn, regardless of how it makes me feel physically or mentally?
- Following a plan (diet) that has been proven to fail in 95% of cases, and also makes *me* feel like a failure?

- Neglecting my mental, physical, and emotional needs in favor of a definition of health that really means "skinny," and is being modeled by people who, 1) May or may not be actually healthy, and, 2) Often don't even look like what I'm seeing because of Photoshop?
- Losing it in the middle of Starbucks because my drink order got messed up and a sip of dairy is the end of the world?

Over time, these things seemed less and less healthy to me.

As I discovered intuitive eating, developed supportive coping mechanisms, and learned how to take care of myself, I was exposed to new and different ways to approach my body, food, and movement. I was able to ask myself, do these new ways seem healthy? Does true health look like:

- Taking intentional steps to reconnect with my body's natural signals?
- Learning to speak with compassion, honesty, and respect to myself?
- Trading judgment for curiosity so that I can learn more about myself and my needs?
- Developing the skills to nourish myself?
- Balancing my physical, emotional, mental, social, and spiritual needs depending on the situation and circumstances?
- Feeling safe — rather than terrified or triggered — around food, so that I can make empowered and calm choices about what would feel good and right for *me*?
- Listening to my body's messages about what I need rather than someone else who knows nothing about me personally?
- Practicing flexibility?
- Looking at overall well being to indicate health?
- Moving my body in ways that enhance and support me and the life I desire to live?

- Experiencing joy, presence, flexibility, and connection in ways that honor who I am?
- Caring for my body TODAY, regardless of whether certain "conditions" (like being a certain weight) have been met (i.e. unconditional self-care)?
- Learning to embrace my body's healthiest and happiest shape and size with the understanding that bodies are made to change?
- NOT losing it in the middle of Starbucks because my drink order got messed up and NOT thinking that a sip of dairy is the end of the world?

Ah, yes. Those things started to sound more like the health I wanted to experience.

A Stuffed Lace Sausage

It was night three of our Canadian honeymoon.

If you're wondering, "Canada, eh?" First … ha, ha. Second, Tim and I had planned to spend the post-wedding week in a cabana in Belize, but a last-minute hurricane hit, so we got creative and headed north.

We did all the obnoxious, romantic things. We held hands across the café table, chatted over candlelight, sipped wine, shared oysters, and fed each other French fries. We laughed about our favorite wedding weekend memories and both agreed we wouldn't change a thing. We dreamed up the future, from where we'd travel to what we'd name our kids. And when dinner ended, we gathered up the bags from our antiquing adventures earlier that day and tipsily stumbled on the cobblestone Quebec City streets back to Le Château Frontenac. Once in our room, Tim opened the window to let in the crisp October air and the sounds of the saxophone player from the boardwalk below.

IS MY LIFE A NANCY MEYER'S MOVIE?

More like Woody Allen.

Everything on the outside looked great. But inside, things were a mess. I felt so uncomfortable. I could feel my jeans squeezing my stomach more tightly than they had before dinner, and all I could think about what was how badly I wanted to cry.

Every time Tim gave me a kiss or put his hand on my lower back, my skin crawled. Not because of him, but because I thought *I hope he can't feel how gross I got tonight.* Never has "It's not you, it's me!" felt more true.

In my mind I was obsessing over the countless fries I ate at dinner; the unaccounted calories in the decadent dipping sauces; the "too many" glasses of wine I drank; and how I was going to have to get up at 5:30 AM to try to run off the damage (*with a hangover, ugh*).

I was mad at myself for not feeling happy about everything that was actually so good. Interestingly enough, being mad at yourself for not being happy enough actually does not increase happiness. I felt heavy and frantic.

I had to get some space because spazzing requires more room than one would think.

I grabbed some black lingerie and escaped to the bathroom with the promise to return in "something special" (wink wink).

Alone in the bathroom, I stripped off my clothes in front of the mirror. I zeroed in on the large zit on my face. *Probably from the fried food at dinner*, I thought. I looked intensely at my soft post-dinner belly. *Definitely from the fried food at dinner,* I confirmed. I continued to examine and critique my appearance for such a long time that Tim finally called into the bathroom, "Everything OK in there?"

"Yeah! Everything is good! Almost done."

Everything was *not* good. And I certainly wasn't almost done.

71

I pulled the lingerie over my head and looked in the mirror. If looking at yourself naked when you're feeling self-conscious makes you feel badly about yourself, I can confirm that looking at yourself in lingerie makes you feel even worse. I looked nothing like the underwear models I saw walking the Victoria's Secret runway show. I did not appear to have a sexy secret. I felt like a sausage in black lace. *I can't possibly go out there looking like a stuffed lace sausage, can I?!*

I pulled at the underwear cutting into my skin. That didn't help the overall aesthetic, so I sat on the bathroom floor and cried. Well, crying is a nice way to put what I did. Bawling. Wailing. Weeping. I might have been drooling, but since nobody was in the bathroom to confirm, let's pretend I wasn't.

Discretion is not my thing, and unsurprisingly, Tim heard my sobs.

He knocked softly on the locked door and asked, "What's wrong, Sim?"

"EVERYTHING." I sobbed. It felt like the truth.

I told him how I felt hideous, unlovable, and disgusting. I shared how much guilt I had about dinner. And about most dinners, for that matter. How I panicked if I couldn't exercise every day. "If I could just get to my goal weight, things would be better," I promised.

I had never told anyone how I felt about myself in such an honest way, but that night I let it all out through the bathroom door.

I cried and cried and cried until I had squeezed all the water out of my face. Then, empty, I traded tears for dry heaving, which involved crinkling up my face and making noises like a cat in heat. I made sure to look in the mirror while I did this, too, because direct eye contact with yourself is where the energy to continue emoting comes from.

When all the tears had been cried and all the dry heaves had been heaved, I finally unlocked the bathroom door. Tim greeted me, the puffy-eyed lace-wrapped sausage, with a hug. This time, my skin didn't crawl.

While holding me close, he whispered in my ear, "Sim, it doesn't have to be like this. These things you're saying about yourself are scary. Something needs to change."

I knew what he was saying was true. But sometimes true is scary. I had no idea how I was going to change. I knew there were so many good things in my life, but I couldn't enjoy any of them.

Brené Brown says, "You can't numb those hard feelings without numbing the other affects, our emotions. You cannot selectively numb. So when we numb those [hard feelings], we numb joy, we numb gratitude, we numb happiness."

I had spent so long trying to make the hard stuff go away to feel lovable. I was numb but I finally realized it. I was ready for something to change.

Living With a Judgmental Bully

At a dinner party a few weeks before Osh's first birthday, we were playing the question game. Christiana asked us all to answer, "When was the time in your life when you were the worst?" Mine, without a doubt, was 7th grade. Christiana 100% agreed. You can't hide anything from your sister. We unanimously agreed on this time in my life because I was, well, mean.

I'd spent the first dozen years of my life feeling like the annoying one. I guess we're all a little bit of our 12-year-old selves, because at 30-something, this is still a real fear for me.

Back to 7th grade, when a group of girls who I thought were super cool started talking to me. I was in shock. I looked up to them so much. I wanted them to hang out with me, and suddenly, it was happening.

It felt more magical than Disney World!

As middle school kids do, we were all trying to figure out who we were and where our place was in the world. And by "world," I mean the cafeteria. We were going out with boys for the first time, which as I'm sure you know, is middle school slang for being "boyfriend and girlfriend" while literally going nowhere. We were trying out different styles, like butterfly hair clips and full-face glitter applied with a roller ball stick. We were finding our people.

Other than sitting together at lunchtime, a good way to let people know that they were your people was to invite them over for sleepovers where you did choreographed dances, snuck R-rated movies into the VCR, and drank neon beverages like Surge and Mountain Dew in quantities that should've been illegal.

There were plenty of times where I wasn't invited to a sleepover. During those times, I would feel sad and left out. I would pray, *Please God, let me have friends! Please let them like me! I don't want to be alone.* There were also plenty of times where I was on the other side, inviting a few girls over and leaving others out.

There is one very specific time where this happened that will stay burnt into my brain for eternity. A group of us got together to hang out and decided to go ice skating on a pond where we knew another girl (who was *not* invited) would see us. I don't know why we thought it was a good idea to go out of our way to make someone feel left out, but I would venture a guess that it was so that we could feel left IN.

It didn't work. I felt awful. And 20 years later, I still feel awful.

It never feels good to be left out. But, what I learned skating around on that winter day was that it didn't feel good to be left in at someone else's expense, either. I went home that night feeling so empty and sad. I felt disappointed in myself and wished I could have a do-over.

Why would you be so mean to someone who was your friend? I asked myself. Somewhere deep down, I was afraid that if everyone else was invited, there might not be any room for me.

I would love to tell you that I left my inner mean girl on the ice in 7th grade. But I didn't. I turned all the meanness onto myself.

I called myself ugly and annoying and not good enough. I put myself in situations that reinforced these beliefs and then berated myself when they ended badly. I was in a constant search of validation — from teachers, grades, guys, friends, family, work, photos, and the scale — and I was left feeling like I had messed something up anytime I didn't get it. I told myself that my A's should be A+'s, my stomach should be flatter, and my hair straighter. If someone was in a bad mood, I guessed it was my fault. When things didn't go according to plan, I assumed I was being punished. So then I would punish myself for being the kind of person who deserved to be punished in the first place. I would think mean things, ignore what my body needed, make myself run when it hurt, withhold food, and refuse human interaction.

I would shut down and shut off.

If I had been treating anyone other than myself like this, I would have called it an abusive relationship.

Try harder, be nicer, get skinnier, do better. BE BETTER.

It was exhausting living with a judgmental bully. It doesn't do great things for your confidence.

After my honeymoon, I knew things had to change.

So, with zero confidence, a lot of anxiety, and a little depression, I started to work on myself. This wasn't another intense diet or exercise-training plan. I was working with my first health coach and getting into regular therapy. In the beginning, I thought I had work to do on my relationship with food. I just wanted to stop hating myself anytime I ate something other than a plate of spinach with a side of green tea. I learned that it wasn't about food at all.

My relationship with food was a mirror to my relationship with everything else. Especially the one I had with myself.

Intuitive eating, confidence building, freedom from people pleasing, and body image work are all related to my relationship with myself. In my experience, deep relationships require loving yet honest communication, trust, quality time, and connection. I hadn't had any of those things with myself in a really long time, so I had to start from the ground up. Since I had no idea how to talk to myself with any voice other than my judgmental inner Regina George, it was like learning a whole new language (I was always better at math).

Mother Theresa said, "If you judge people, you have no time to love them."

I hadn't loved myself in quite a while.

My therapist had me do a lot of writing exercises during our early work. The most profound was a series of letters she encouraged me to write. I wrote the first letter from my mind to my body. In it, I shared everything I wanted my body to know. I asked my body why she was gaining weight even though I was trying everything to keep her small. I asked her why she was always rebelling against me. *Why can't you just cooperate? Do the right thing? I'm trying SO hard.* Why wouldn't she just do what I was trying to make her do? If she did, I told her that I could finally relax a bit and not have to work so hard all the time.

The second letter I wrote was a reply from my body to my mind. I was afraid my body would have nothing to say. But when I put pen to paper, I couldn't believe how many words flowed out.

You're hurting me. You've abandoned me. Sometimes you starve me and I get scared. I don't feel safe. Sometimes you stuff me so full of food,

I want to burst. You push me so hard and I ache. You say mean things to me and they make me sad. I am trying my best. I love you so much and I'm trying to make everything OK. I know why you're doing this. You just want to be loved. You think all the things you're doing are going to make you more lovable. But listen: Do you remember when you were mean to your friend in 7ᵗʰ grade because you thought it would make you feel like you belonged? And then it didn't work at all? Well, guess what: This isn't working either. It didn't work then, it hasn't been working for years, and it isn't working now. Nothing you're doing is making you more lovable. It won't make you enough. **Because you already are those things.** *You are lovable. You are enough. So, what I need from you is some kindness. Some gentleness. Some compassion. Some care. Because mean isn't working here – it never has and it never will. Come home.*

At our next session, I shared that I figured it all out. I figured she would say, "OK!" and teach me how not to care if people loved me or not. Instead, she asked me what it felt like to think about someone not liking me.

"Scary," I told her.

We dug a little deeper. What felt so scary about it was that if I said the wrong thing or did the wrong thing and someone didn't like me, then he or she would leave.

"Ah, so you think that if you aren't perfect, people will leave you?"

Yes, that is exactly what I thought.

"Who has left you in your life when you said or did the wrong thing?"

I honestly couldn't think of anyone. I mean, I definitely had relationships that ended, but in hindsight it didn't feel like the ends were my fault. It felt like those relationships were meant to come to an end.

"I don't know, I guess I can't think of anybody."

"Hm. What about *you*?" she asked.

And she was so right. I was the one that left myself when I wasn't perfect.

I was the one who said awful things to myself, who punished myself, and who checked out. I was the one who looked for anything to numb pain or avoid discomfort: too much food, too little food, online shopping, running more miles, reading celebrity gossip. Whatever I could get my hands on. Whatever would help me escape.

I was the only one who left when I wasn't perfect.

I had to learn how to stay.

SHEDDING THE SHOULDS / TWO BANANAS, REAL BACON, AND HAIRY ARMPITS

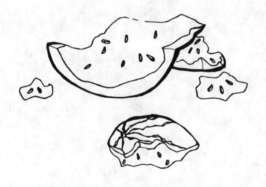

The Other Side of My Goal Weight

Can any random person declare an epidemic? Because I think we've got one.

I spent more than a decade believing that real life was on the other side of my goal weight. I had a whole list of things I would be able to do once I "lost the weight." Or got the job. Or got engaged. Or got married. Or made more money. Or owned a home. Or did any number of things that actually aren't requirements for having fun.

I thought it was only me.

But now, when I look around, I see it wasn't. Everywhere I look, I see women hating their bodies. I hear them putting off living their lives until they lose weight. They believe they need to lose 10, 20, or 30 pounds just to have permission to enjoy their lives! To wear shorts! To go on vacation! To eat a carb!

We are led to believe that we have to live up to impossible standards to be loved or to be "enough." We download it as truth, and then teach it to each other.

We are told to be nice, sweet, popular, and likable.

Be smart, but not in an intimidating way.

Be fit, but not masculine.

Be pretty, but in a natural way. (And it's totally OK to spend thousands of dollars in cosmetics and procedures to look "natural.")

Be sexy, but not slutty.

Work really hard at whatever you do, but make sure not to step on anybody's toes while climbing to the top in those super high, super uncomfortable heels.

Get beach-ready, bikini-ready, wedding-ready, reunion-ready. And definitely get that "pre-baby body" back ASAP.

Be sensitive but not emotional. Definitely don't be too emotional.

Be the caregiver and the "yes" (wo)man.

Even strangers on the street tell us to "smile!"

Please, strangers, stop doing this.

When we "fall short," we're told that we're the problem, not the impossible and often contradictory standards. We're encouraged to buy something else to help us get a little closer next time.

We're not taught how to practice self-compassion through difficult situations, feel our feelings, value our inherent worth, trust ourselves, feed our bodies, and connect with who we are. Instead, we're taught to fear ourselves, please everyone else, and look for validation externally in all areas of life. We're told every single day — by teachers, "gurus," and the media — that we need to practice more willpower, have more control, and follow more rules. We're told that our bodies can't be trusted and must be fixed.

Honestly, I bought into all of it, monetarily and emotionally. I purchased every magazine, book, and program that claimed to hold the secret to my salvation. I spent hours of my life Googling how to be more like Jessica — Simpson, Biel, or Alba would have been fine with me! I crafted intricate meal plans, created epic schedule spreadsheets, counted calories, measured food, and got up early. I cleansed and volunteered and ran marathons and got A's in school.

I did it all! I even smiled while I was doing it. My life was full of what I "should" do, and guilt around anything I "shouldn't" do.

I was wound so tightly that if the smallest thing didn't go according to plan, I'd be set off into a tailspin. You know the crusty end slices on a loaf of bread? Yeah, you better pray that I didn't go to make my morning toast only to find those slices. It was like the apocalypse in my kitchen.

WHY ME?! WHY ARE THERE NO REGULAR SLICES OF BREAD? I AM SO DESTINED FOR FAILURE THAT EVEN TOAST KNOWS!

Glennon Melton Doyle says that people who need help sometimes look a lot like people who don't. I think she was talking about me when she wrote that. Only I had no idea what "help" actually looked like. So, when I got home from my honeymoon, I Googled it.

After Googling some things about "no more diets" and "how to not hate myself anymore," I came across the website for a health coach who was located in Columbus, Ohio. At the time, I had no idea what a health coach was. But she looked like an angel radiating joy and light (all the things I was definitely not radiating). Clearly she knew something I didn't. She also talked about how she could help women feel great in their bodies, create confidence, and live a high-vibe life.

Perfect, I thought. *I want to have confidence! I want to feel great in my body! I want to vibe high!*

I felt equal parts hopeful and terrified as I clicked the "Submit" button and requested a consultation.

In my 30-minute call with her, I proceeded to cry hysterically while explaining the desperation, frustration, and general state of freaking out that afflicted me (see: above epidemic). I have no clue if she could hear a single thing I was saying, but she promised she could help me. So I signed up.

At the time, I thought I was about to receive a step-by-step prescription for success. But, not like a diet ... different. More high-vibe. Yes! A high-vibe anti-diet that would tell me exactly what to do, eat, think, and say. I imagined her sharing some special recipe for a green smoothie that would change my world. It would probably have some soaked seed I had never heard of or an exotic flower powder only the wellness insiders knew about. Or maybe she would give me a mantra I could recite in the mirror to suddenly see an underwear model staring back at me. Sort of like when you play "Bloody Mary" in the bathroom as kids, only more fun and less terrifying since I would see Gisele, not a dead person. Basically, I wanted my health coach to tell me exactly what she did in her life so I could mimic her behavior and become her.

I'm a mere six months from becoming a tall, long-legged blonde, I encouraged myself. *This is going to be great!*

Days later, it was time for my first official health coaching session and I couldn't wait to get started so she could tell me exactly what I should do with my life. I was READY! But a few minutes into our call, something unexpected happened. Rather than tell me what to do, she asked me a question.

With kindness and genuine curiosity in her voice, she asked, "Love, what do you enjoy?"

Crickets.

"What do I enjoy?" At a loss for words, I just repeated hers back to her.

"Yeah! What foods do you enjoy eating? Or what activities do you enjoy doing? What brings you joy?"

I thought about it for a second. Then for a few more. Then for a few more. And I came up with a big nothing.

"Uh, I honestly don't know." I shared, embarrassed that I was a 25-year-old who didn't even know what I liked. "I know what I think I should eat. I know what I think I should do. But I'm not sure if I actually like those things. I just do them because I feel so guilty when I don't. But I guess not feeling guilty is different than actually enjoying something. Right?" I asked, not even sure if that was true.

"By the time I finish doing everything I 'should' do, I'm pretty exhausted and usually watch reality TV until I pass out." I kept going.

"Hmmm. Yes." She said, giving me a little more space to process what I'd just shared.

I came to the realization that I didn't actually enjoy much of anything. I didn't even really remember what joy felt like, since all my experiences were so clouded by guilt and fear of failure.

She encouraged me to try a two-week experiment of "shedding the shoulds."

For two weeks, I committed to erasing the words "should" and "shouldn't" from my vocabulary and trying things I might enjoy. I would report back with what I actually liked. And also what I didn't.

I was freaking terrified. When you've spent years of your life feeling like you weren't safe to trust what feels good, joy is scary! I was terrified I would go off the rails. I was terrified that I was missing the joy gene. I was terrified that I would eat the wrong thing and my body would implode. I was terrified I would fail.

But my health coach reminded me of something: I couldn't fail. I didn't believe her (see: above epidemic), but I promised to do my best. Off I went.

Over the next two weeks, I heard the words *should* and *shouldn't* no less than a thousand times in my head. But each time I heard the word, I imagined myself clicking the "delete" key on my brain's keyboard and clearing it from my mind. In the empty place I would ask, *What do you think you would ENJOY doing here, instead?*

Since I had no clue how to have fun anymore, I thought about what other people seemed to do for fun and what I used to do for fun before I accidentally unlearned how to have it.

I tried those things first.

I read a book. Not a diet book or law journal, but fiction. Oh, the novelty! I ate mac 'n' cheese at dinner for no special reason. I went out for a drink with my friends. And not red wine, either … a cocktail with real booze and syrup! I made out with my husband. I listened to my favorite 90s music and danced alone. I went to a barre class when I would have normally forced myself to go for a run. I ate two bananas in one day and tried real bacon. I went to a coffee shop for a super frothy cappuccino rather than drinking green tea at home. I didn't shave my armpits for four days. I bought jeans that fit.

I was scared but I kept telling myself *It's only two weeks, it's only two weeks, it's only two weeks!*

It turns out, you can learn a lot in two weeks.

I learned that I did, in fact, have functioning taste buds. I was shocked to discover that I actually didn't like the kale smoothie I made each day. It brought me zero joy. It tasted like sweaty feet. You know what didn't taste like sweaty feet? Mac 'n' cheese.

I learned that smiling didn't only happen because it's the socially appropriate moment. Sometimes it happens because a moment is so nice that you just can't help but smile. At the top of the list of moments that are so nice that you just can't help but smile is putting on a pair of jeans that actually fits. Pants that didn't make me feel like I was being stabbed in the abdomen every time I sat down? Game changer. So much joy in not being stabbed in the abdomen.

I learned that I don't have to earn the right to lie down by pushing myself so hard that I have no option but to collapse. Lying down when I was already rested was truly a lovely and enjoyable experience.

I learned that part of re-learning how to enjoy things is trying something only to discover that you don't like it. I learned that not liking something is very different from failure. They are actually completely unrelated. I was safe to not like something! The world did not end!

At our next session, I shared everything I had learned. I shared the things that I enjoyed. I also shared the things that I realized I did not enjoy.

"It's like I'm dating myself!" I told her. "Awkward but fun!"

When we hung up at the end of our phone call, I walked back into the law firm for a few more hours at work. Rather than go into production mode, I took a moment and just sat at my desk. I looked around. I looked out the big window. I looked at the files stacked on my desk. I looked into the hallway. I looked at my computer.

Something felt off.

What is this feeling I'm having? I wondered.

A little empty. A little sad. A little anxious. A little like when I drank that kale smoothie.

Oh crap, I realized. *I don't think I like being a lawyer.*

F-E-A-R

A quote I found on Pinterest told me that the word 'fear' really means:

False
Evidence
Appearing
Real

I wish Pinterest would've told this to my five-year-old self on the night that a wet leaf hit my bedroom window just as I was about to fall asleep. Do you know what a wet leaf looks like when it hits your bedroom window at night?

A HAND! IT LOOKS LIKE A CREEPY WITCH HAND!

I jumped out of my bed faster than you can find cheesy quotes about fear on Pinterest, and bolted down the hallway to my parents' bedroom. And I didn't leave their room until I left for college.

From that terrifying foliage encounter on, I was afraid of the dark. My younger sister also happens to be MUCH braver than me (everyone mistakes her for being older and wiser than me, too). So growing up, I'd send that brave sister up the stairs before bedtime every night to check in my room, under my bed, and in my closet just to make sure the coast was clear. She would report back that my bedroom was safe, but as soon as the lights went out I would forget all those reassurances! I would hear noises, which terrified me. I would hear silence, which terrified me even more. If even the tips of my toes were sticking out of the comforter, I'd panic that that creepy witch was about to grab them and pull me under the bed to never again return.

I didn't want to never again return! I had cereal to eat! Cartoons to watch! Trampolines to jump on! Dolls to play with! I had so much life ahead of me!

From my perspective, there was only one logical option. I was forced to sleep in bed with my parents. Or sometimes on their floor. Or sometimes on the floor right outside of their bedroom on nights when they were really trying to teach me to sleep in my own bedroom again. Or probably, and more likely, just trying to have some sex. I did this all the way through high school.

THIS IS NOT A DRILL! I did not sleep alone until I went to college. And I didn't really sleep alone then either because ROOMMATES! When everyone else in the dorm was complaining about missing personal space, I was silently celebrating.

I wouldn't call myself a fearful person. I just happen to be a person with a long list of things that have made me feel fear. I wouldn't say I have issues with denial either.

In addition to the usual suspects, like the dark, shark attacks, and "Hunger Games" becoming real life, there have been some less usual suspects that have made me feel pretty afraid in the past. Like intuitive eating. Well, less intuitive eating and more the absence of dieting.

THAT was scary. I was terrified to give up dieting.

In their groundbreaking book "Intuitive Eating," Evelyn Tribole and Elyse Resch define intuitive eaters as those who "march to their inner hunger signals, and eat whatever they choose without experiencing guilt or ethical dilemma." They go on to outline the 10 principles of intuitive eating to help heal from the diet mentality, tune into the body's biological signals, and honor those signals from a place of self-trust.

The first and foundational principle of intuitive eating is to reject the diet mentality.

When I read the book, it made perfect sense. I couldn't help but nod my head furiously as I read each page. Deep down, I believed that intuitive eating was the way I was meant to relate to food. But everytime I re-read that first principle, I was filled with fear.

Do I have to reject it? Or can I just skip past that one and embrace principles two through 10? I wondered.

I was craving change but resisting the release that needed to happen to set it in motion. I clung to my restrictive, controlling food behaviors until a very wise women who just so happens to be an amazing coach and also my mom asked me, "What's the really good reason you don't want to give up dieting?"

"I mean I don't diet. I just eat SUPER clean and healthy," I replied. Yep. Zero issues with denial.

"OK, call it whatever you want. What's the really good reason that you don't want to give up SUPER clean and healthy eating?"

I thought to myself *BECAUSE IT'S SUPER CLEAN AND HEALTHY, AND I DON'T WANT TO BE DIRTY AND UNHEALTHY!*

But what I said out loud was, "Uhhhh. I'm not sure I understand the question."

"What are you afraid might happen if you give up these controlling and obsessive behaviors? Why don't you want to give them up?"

Until that point, my every thought was consumed with weight loss. I spent all my time thinking about my weight. Thinking about losing weight. Thinking about how to lose the weight. Doing the things I thought would help me lose weight. Working out to lose the weight. Thinking about what foods I should eat to lose weight. Imagining what clothes I would wear if I could just lose a little more weight. Researching nutrition, detoxes, "secret weight loss solutions," and celebrity tricks for weight loss. Thinking about what I would buy at the grocery store to eat what I needed to eat to lose weight. Prepping the food that I needed to eat those things. Measuring the food I planned to eat. Eating the food and immediately thinking about the next thing I would eat. Feeling hopeful that the next diet — er, the next "super clean and healthy eating plan" — would be the one that would make my dreams come true. Hating myself when I broke a rule or fell off the wagon or did something "bad." Criticizing myself, comparing myself to others, and falling short over and over again.

I thought about the countless hours and I realized it was a lot of time. It was a full-on hobby! No, it was more like a full-time job.

If I rejected the diet mentality, I realized I had no clue what I would do with my time, my thoughts, or my life. And this was my very good reason (aka my very big f-e-a-r) that kept me from making a change. I was afraid because "losing weight" was my ~~hobby~~ life.

"I'm scared," I said. "If I'm not thinking about losing weight, what will I think about all the time?!"

False
Evidence
Appearing
Real

"Well, there's only one way to find out, right?" She told me.

She was right. *SHE'S ALWAYS RIGHT.*

So, I did it. I felt my fear and did it anyway. I ditched the diet mentality and started to live my life. At first, I had to remind myself 10,000 times a day, *I don't diet anymore! That's not what I do!* Because, at first, I wanted to diet again, 10,000 times a day.

Instead, I asked myself, *If there was nothing about me to fix, if weight loss wasn't my goal, what would I do today? What would I say "yes" to?* And then, I'd do that thing. I'd say "yes" to that thing.

At first, it was hard. I didn't know what I liked. I didn't know how to be in my own mind without focusing on my rules. I didn't know how to move forward as if I was already enough. But I kept reminding myself, *You're going to discover things that make you smile. You're going to feel relaxed. You're going to have so many wonderful things to think about that you won't believe you ever filled so much of your mind with those rules.*

And, unlike the fears, these thoughts actually turned out to be true.

Here is a non-exhaustive list of things that fill my heart, thoughts, and life today:

- Stories in books that are not about diets
- Laughing a lot
- Really listening to people when they share things with me
- Hugs that don't make my skin squirm
- Honesty
- Talking to God
- Playing board games
- Eating donuts with friends
- Snuggling dogs
- Crying tears

- Smiling at strangers
- The smell of coffee
- The smell of fresh air
- The smell of my baby boy
- Standing in the ocean
- Dreams for my business
- Dreams for my family
- Going after my dreams
- Comforting myself when something I really hoped for doesn't happen
- Celebrating when something I hadn't even thought to hope for does
- Opening up to the people I trust about things that feel hard for me
- Thinking about other people more than myself
- Doing little things to help others
- Meeting new people
- Writing
- Being in love
- Really SEEING the people I love (including myself)

I honestly thought that I would never know what made me happy. A part of me believed that I wasn't even capable of feeling joy. I thought that if I let go of my weight loss goals that my body would turn into something that I hated (even more than I already did). But the opposite happened. I *did* find things that make me happy, I *can* feel joy, and I *have* learned to love myself. Just like the creepy witch hand that turned out to be a wet leaf on my window, my mind was playing tricks on me. It was simply false evidence appearing real.

The Best Watermelon of My Life

When I first started eating intuitively, I was terrified to *feel* anything around food. I didn't want to get too excited because I worried that I wouldn't be able to make myself stop eating when I was full. I didn't want to feel too much pleasure because I feared the same.

I was so used to using food as an emotional coping mechanism that I no longer felt safe experiencing emotion around it. If it were delicious and I was really enjoying each bite, how would I ever make myself put down the fork? NO WAY! I didn't believe it was possible to feel emotions and do a good job eating intuitively at the same time.

I'd been learning about intuitive eating for a few months, digging into literature, podcasts, and articles. The more I read, the more the concepts made sense. It was the first time I'd truly believed in an approach to food. With the diets and detox plans I'd tried before, I simply *hoped* they would work (and by "work," I meant make me skinnier). With intuitive eating, it was different. I really *believed* that it could work (and by "work," I meant help me to stop losing my mind around food).

Because I believed it could work, I naturally wanted it to work for me. I didn't want to mess it up. There was a part of me that still felt that I had failed at my years of weight loss attempts. I didn't want to fail this. It felt like the real deal, and I wanted to do it right.

I ate intuitively just like I dieted. I followed the rules. I wanted to do it perfectly. I wanted to be perfectly free around food. I wanted to perfectly listen to my body. I heavily monitored my hunger pangs, I ate as slowly as possible so I could notice my fullness cues, and I worked hard to make all "off limits" foods "on limits" again. I ate at the table away from distractions. I had ice cream for breakfast if that was what I wanted.

BUT I DIDN'T GET EXCITED ABOUT IT.

What is the point of ice cream for breakfast if you can't even get excited about it? I felt my inner voice ask.

SHHHHH. JUST STOP WHEN YOU'RE FULL! I barked back.

It was during this eat-exactly-when-hungry-stop-right-when-full time that I went to stay with my sweet grandma for a week in Pittsburgh. She was getting ready to move into a nursing home, but it was going to be a few days until her room was ready. She couldn't be on her own, so I got to be with her until it was time to move.

My grandma was someone to meet. She was just shy of five feet tall, shrinking with every passing year. Thanks to timely sarcasm and random bursts of curse words, she was funny without even trying. My birthday cards from her and my grandpa each year would read, "Credit card debt is at an all time high, global warming is real, and college tuition continues to rise. Happy birthday. We love you." *UPLIFTING!* Her hugs were strong, her brownies generously iced, and she played one hell of a game of Spoons.

On top of being a hilarious brownie genius, she was also stubborn: a trait that she abundantly passed down through my mom to me. The week that I stayed with her, this burly characteristic may or may not have been to blame for a little head-butting between us (it definitely was). My grandma didn't want to leave her chair. I did everything I could to get her to wheel onto the front porch for some fresh air (she wouldn't budge). My grandma complained that she was bored. I did everything I could to get her to do an activity (she shot them all down). My grandma didn't want to eat anything. I did everything I could to make her eat something (she pushed it all away). It went on and on and on like this. I was losing my mind! She was losing her mind!

Two stubborn people does not a flexible person make.

So, on a random Wednesday afternoon when she said, "Simi, I want watermelon. Take me to the farmers market to get watermelon," I squealed, "YOU GOT IT!!!"

We were going to have something to do, get some fresh air, AND she would eat. This was the definition of winning.

I got her dressed in "that pair of black slacks and soft button down black sweater" that she insisted on. In July. But you know what? I wasn't going to argue because this was no time to rock the boat. I dressed her like she was headed to a funeral in November and we headed to the farmers market to get some juicy watermelon.

The ride to the market was a dream. I pushed her wheelchair downhill the entire way. Easy peasy! We were flying free with the wind in our face and the sun on our backs. At the market, she found a melon that was worthy of our three dollars and it was time to roll on home. Only, I had put the cash in my pocket and forgot a bag. The farmers market didn't have any bags. We had nowhere to put the melon.

I tried holding it in one hand but the walk home was an intense uphill climb and I didn't have enough strength to push the wheelchair with only one hand. She was forced to sit with it on her legs while I started hauling us up the hill toward home. I mentioned my grandma was short, but did I mention she was tiny? This watermelon probably weighed more than her lower half. The sun was BEATING US in the face.

"Simi! My legs are so hot! These black pants feel like they are on fire!" she yelled back at me.

"OK, grandma! We will take them off as soon as we get home!" I said through gritted teeth.

I KNEW THOSE FRICKIN' PANTS WERE A BAD CHOICE!

"This watermelon is so heavy! I can hardly hold onto it!" she moaned at me. Sweat was dripping into my eyes and my body was practically horizontal trying to push her, hot pants and all, up the hill.

"It's slipping!" she shrieked.

"Just hang on, grandma! We're almost there!" I shrieked back.

The watermelon smashed onto the ground. Juice splashed my ankles.

"There it goes." She stated, matter-of-factly.

OH REALLY? THANK YOU I HADN'T REALIZED WHAT JUST HAPPENED.

At this point I was sweating more than someone in a hot yoga class. I was also decidedly less zen. I rolled grandma into the grass off the sidewalk and hit her break. Looking at the splattered watermelon, I wanted to cry.

"I really wanted watermelon," she informed me.

"Yeah, me too," I replied.

My grandmother was a very hygienic person. Her home had two bathrooms in it. The one on the first floor was full of pink floral curtains and towels. Not a toothbrush was out of place, not a watermark on the mirror, not a smudge of toothpaste in the sink. The other bathroom, which everyone but my grandma used, was in the basement. So you can imagine her disgust when I asked her, "Do you want a piece?" while pointing to the ground.

Her appalled facial expression told me that, no, she did not want a piece of the watermelon. But I didn't let that stop me. I reached down onto the hot concrete and grabbed a jagged chunk of watermelon. I bit right in, letting the juice drip down my face. I just spent three bucks at a farmers market and wasn't about to lose out on our investment.

IT TASTED SO GOOD.

"Grandma, this tastes so good. It's the best watermelon of my life. You've got to try a bite." I shared, shoving a piece into her face. Confused, she took a bite.

"Oh my!" she said. "This is refreshing! Put a little of that watermelon juice on my thighs to cool them off!"

We sat there, her in her wheelchair and me on the grass, eating a dirty watermelon while we laughed our heads off.

THIS DIRTY WATERMELON IS SO GOOD HAHAHA. WE ARE SO HOT HAHAHA. LOOK AT THIS MESS HAHAHA.

I was so tired and so hot and so over it that I just let myself be in the moment. I let myself enjoy. I let myself have fun. I let myself laugh and feel silly and experience pleasure. And I survived! I didn't eat until I exploded. I didn't try and swallow the rind of the watermelon. I didn't take a bite of my grandma's arm. I just ate delicious watermelon until I was full and then I stopped.

A few minutes later, my grandma said, "OK Simi, my legs are really very hot. Can we go home now?"

So we did. I took her home and got her out of those November funeral pants and we hung out in our underwear while we laid on her bed under the fan.

My grandma is in heaven now and I think about her every time I eat watermelon. I think about how much connection that food brought us. I don't remember exactly what that watermelon tasted like anymore, but I will never forget how much fun we had eating it together.

Taking Up Space

"What's the worst thing someone could say about you?" my mentor asked me. I could think of way more than one thing. I rattled off my list:

You are a burden.
You are annoying.
You are selfish.
You are mean.
You let me down.
You are needy.
You are a bitch.

I cried on the phone as I shared these with her. Just saying the words, one after the other, was painful to my heart. These are the worst things that someone could say to me.

For as long as I could remember, I wanted to be everything that everyone needed and nothing that they didn't. I feared people would think those exact thoughts about me, and I desperately strived to be the opposite. I wanted to say everything that people wanted to hear, and nothing that they didn't. I wanted to say "yes" to every request so that I never had to let anybody down. I didn't want to need things from people because they might get annoyed with me and leave. I didn't want to do the wrong thing, say the wrong thing, or be the wrong thing because they might think I was a bitch, or selfish, or a burden. And then leave.

One of the reasons I loved losing weight was because it made me smaller. The smaller I was, the less space I took up. The less space I took up, the less I would bother people. At least that's what I believed. Sometimes I dreamed of shrinking down so small that I never had to bother anybody ever again. That sounded less stressful than worrying about being good all the time.

Another reason I loved losing weight was because people told me that I was doing a good job. It made me feel like I was doing something right in the world. The smaller I got, the more people reinforced it. When I would gain weight, people would stop complimenting me. When they weren't telling me that I was good, I wasn't sure if I *was* good anymore.

The absence of the validation felt like the presence of my worst fears: *I was bad, I was wrong, and people thought all those horrible things about me.*

It took me a long time to realize we live in a culture that values "thin" above anything else a woman can be. As a whole, our culture places thin above health, and promotes it at all costs and in unhealthy ways. It glamorizes eating disorders: prescribing restriction as "balance," praising weight loss, and shaming fat people. Diet culture is so ingrained in our society that it often goes unnoticed. Over time, it has become sneakier and sneakier. Diets aren't like they were in the 90s. In the 90s, people were honest about dieting. In the 90s people said, "I am drinking only grapefruit juice or eating only cabbage soup so I can wear smaller jeans." Now, people say, "I am drinking only grapefruit juice or eating only cabbage soup to cleanse my body and create abundant wellness and live my best life."

I miss the 90s, where at least people were honest about their diets and Leonardo DiCaprio was my boyfriend (in my mind).

I'll never forget watching "Romeo and Juliet," falling more deeply in love with Leonardo DiCaprio after each scene. It was 1996, and at the age of 10, I fell so hard. There was no reasoning with me. I went to school hoping he would randomly walk through the doors to take me on a date. I opened my locker praying there would be a note from him. I dreamed of our future together, frolicking from one awards show to another and making out in the limo in between events. I wrote him letters. I made out with posters of him. My mom even caught me fake interviewing myself once:

"So, what's it like being Leo's girlfriend?" I asked myself in my best interviewer's voice.

"It's truly magical. We are so in love. He is the love of my life and loves me a lot I think. He's a good kisser, too." I responded in my best girlfriend voice.

He was the center of my world.

At that point, my heart had never really been broken, so I was all in. There was nothing holding me back from giving everything I had to Leo. This was the beauty of my first love – it was fearless.

I don't generally think it's a good idea to put words in other people's mouths or thoughts in their minds, but if I had to guess I would say that the level of adoration was not entirely reciprocated.

"IF LOVING HIM IS WRONG I DON'T WANT TO BE RIGHT! I JUST LOVE HIM! Why can't you get that, MOM?!" I'd yell hysterically, throwing myself on the living room floor.

When it didn't work out (shocker), I remember thinking the reason must have been because I was not as skinny as Claire Danes in "Romeo and Juliet."

That's what I concluded at the age of 10. It had nothing to do with the fact that we had never met. Or that I was being creepy. Or that my heart was destined for another blonde man in the future named Tim. Nope, none of those reasons. I knew it was my weight.

And that line of reasoning didn't end there. I continued to believe that the smaller I was, the better I was. This was a message fed to me over and over again by culture and, later in life, by the comments I did (or did not) receive from people around me.

Smaller was good. Bigger was not.

I wanted to be good.

What I didn't realize then, or for many years after, was that people will tell us what we should do. What we should say. Who we should be. What we should eat. What values we should have. But that doesn't mean we have to be those things or say those words or hold those values. We get to choose all of those things for ourselves.

I had to ask myself, *Am I just going to live my whole life obsessing about my weight? Am I going to die having spent all my time on earth trying to be skinnier? Trying to make other people happy? Trying not to need anything or not to be annoying or not to say the wrong thing? Is this my purpose? Is this who I am?*

No. Surely I am here for more than this. Surely God made me for more than not pissing people off or not taking up too much space. I have a purpose and it is not to be the smallest version of myself.

And because I have chosen who I am (even if it feels scary) and what I will say (even when it feels scary) and what I will value (even when it feels scary), I remind myself each day that I am safe to be me. Each day I remind myself:

I have permission to change. I'm made to change.
I have permission to take up space. I'm made to take up space.
I have permission to need things. I'm made to need things.
I have permission to be me. I'm made to be me.

I Jumped in the Damn Waves

Like clockwork, the moment that a special event or vacation went on the schedule, the inner dialogue would start.

The scale needs to say [INSERT GOAL WEIGHT] by the time I step onto that beach. If I reach that weight, I will be OK.

Two months until vacation. So that would be eight weeks. If I can lose two pounds a week until then, I think everything will be OK when I need to put on that swimsuit.

OK, only one month until vacation. So, I just need to lose four pounds a week until vacation and I think everything will be OK.

Oh no! I only have two weeks until vacation. If I only drink fluids, I think everything will be OK. I'll just have to cancel all of my plans until then, since I won't be able to eat, and buy about 17 pounds of lemons by tomorrow so I can get started.

After eating everything in the world but lemons ...

HOW DID THIS HAPPEN!? Vacation starts tomorrow and I have spent the last two months panic-binge eating. I hate the way I look. I don't deserve to enjoy this vacation after how I've acted. Why can't I get it together? Why do I always do this?

I would then get on the scale and see a number that was not my goal weight. I would see the number and think, *I don't have permission to enjoy this experience. I don't deserve to wear a bathing suit.*

These were the thoughts that used to precede just about every vacation or special event. It happened before weddings, trips to the beach, and even a dinner with a friend who I hadn't seen for a while. Once there, I was in hyper-hide mode.

What is the quickest way to get to the beach, strip off my cover-up, and lay on my back before anyone sees?

Is it possible to hide my stomach with my book while I pretend to read?

Suck in suck in suck in.

Walk slooooooooowly Sim, so your thighs jiggle less on the way to the water.

Pull up the bottoms on the swimsuit to hold in your stomach … oh no! That made your whole butt fall out!

PLEASE don't let me be in that photo they just took. I don't want anybody to see me like this!

I wish I looked like her. Her legs are so much smaller than mine. Her stomach is so much flatter. Look at how she can play beach volleyball and have so much fun, while I'm stuck laying here trying not to breathe or move. I wonder how many lemons I need to drink to look like that? Maybe by my next vacation I can get there. How many weeks would that be? Like 30? So, if I lost a few pounds a week drinking only lemons for 30 weeks …

I would come home from most of these trips or weekend celebrations feeling even worse about myself than when I left. Of course I wanted to stop comparing myself to other people, but I assumed that it could only happen when I looked "as good" or "better" than them (at the time, in my mind, this meant "as thin" or "thinner"). I was insecure about my body and it felt really crappy to live in that place. I was desperate and thought that comparing myself to others might help because it would "motivate" me to be better (aka thinner).

It did not work. The more I tried to get my body to a place where I "deserved" to feel comfortable, the more uncomfortable I felt. The harder I sought validation on the outside, the more invalidated I felt. The more I compared myself to others, the more insecure I felt. As long as I was looking to other people or the number on the scale to measure my worth, I was never going to feel worthy.

And then one day I heard someone share a story about a man who had been blind since birth. This man could not see the number on the scale. This person could not see how his body compared to others. This person could not see his own reflection. He was totally fine. He was happy. He was confident. He didn't need a number to reassure himself it was OK to live his life, to wear weather-appropriate clothing, or to smile.

This blew my mind. If I could no longer see the number on the scale, compare my body to another woman's, or see my own reflection, how would I gauge how I was doing? How would I know if I had permission to have a good day? To enjoy myself? TO WEAR A SWIMSUIT WHEN IT WAS TIME TO SWIM?!

I would have to learn to accept myself for who I was, deep down inside. I would have to learn to ask myself, *How are you feeling?* — not turn to the scale or the women around me for validation. Rather than the constant quest to discover what I needed to do to *be like her*, I would need to learn to ask, "What do *I* need in this area of *my life* right now?"

My mom always says, "What we live we learn, what we learn we practice, what we practice we become."

Living in a constant state of comparison taught me that it sucked living in a constant state of comparison. But I was stuck there until I learned something new. This is how things work. We are all just doing the best with what we know in any given moment, until we learn more and then do the best we can with that. I realized that someone in this world didn't need to look at the scale or see his body compared to someone else's body to know that he had permission to live a good life in the body that he had. So I decided to practice that instead.

I started asking myself an excessive number of questions (I'm very good at extremes. It's a bit of a superpower). I asked myself multiple times a day, *What do you need in this area of your life? What does your body need? What does your heart need? What is your soul asking for? How do you feel?*

Whenever the old practices would pop up and I would think, *What does she eat to look like that?* or *I should get on the scale to see how I'm doing*, I'd imagine that thought on the gigantic dry erase board in my brain. Then, I would take a big, HUGE eraser and get rid of it. In a bright neon marker, I'd replace it with my new question: *WHAT DO YOU NEED?*

You know what never came up when I asked what I truly needed?

1. To look like anyone else
2. To be someone else
3. To lose weight
4. To spend more time on the scale
5. To measure my food
6. To say mean things to myself

7. To suck in my stomach
8. To eat only lemons
9. To hide
10. To disappear

What came up instead were things like *connection. Fun. Freedom. Play. Passion. Presence.*

I started to practice those things so that I could become who I needed to be, deep down inside. Rather than laying flat on my back sucking in my stomach on the beach, I JUMPED IN THE DAMN WAVES! I let my swimsuit ride straight up my butt and I let my hair get wet and I drooled from laughing while losing my breath because jumping in the waves is good at taking my breath away. And I didn't worry about the girl playing beach volleyball on the beach because she was practicing what she needed to practice and I was practicing what I needed to practice. I thought that was pretty cool.

Time went on and years passed. Slowly, over time, I became what I practiced. I became more connected, fun, free, playful, passionate, and present.

From time to time, people say things that remind me that not everyone is practicing what I'm practicing and that's OK — because we're all at different places in our journeys. And when, for a brief moment, I think, *Should I be practicing that, too?*, I remind myself of the man who never looked at another body to decide if his body was good enough. And I close my eyes. When my eyes are closed I feel my body from the inside out. I feel what matters. And when I feel what matters, I can feel that nothing about me needs to change.

Ditch the Bra to Feel the Feelings

"Ma ma ma ma," Osh said lovingly to a non-functioning remote from 2005. This was currently his favorite toy, which he refused to go anywhere without. It was a Monday morning and I sat on the floor next to him, sipping my coffee as he continued to confuse me with an inanimate object.

I know every mom thinks her kid is special, but mine actually is: He is a mind reader. The moments when I think something like *The baby is asleep!*, Osh READS MY MIND and wakes up, just to keep me on my toes. As I thought, *This is such a relaxing morning*, Osh started to get annoyed. I took the cue to check the usual suspects.

Dirty diaper? Nope.

Hungry? Nope.

Fever? Nope.

In a few short moments, fussy turned into explosive crying. I can't imagine who he inherited that from. He was clearly unhappy, so I tried to think of ways I could "fix" his mood. I made his stuffed elephant talk. I turned on Grateful Dead (the kid is obsessed with jam band music). I did my best Lisa Turtle impression, dancing "the sprain." I tried to distract him, but being a one-woman show is exhausting.

HOW DO I FIX THIS?! HOW DO I FIX HIM?! I panicked.

But then I caught myself. There have been so many moments in my life where I felt something uncomfortable and my default was to try to fix it, or myself, or both. And now, in default mode, I was trying to do it to Osh, too.

When feelings that were tougher for me to experience, like rejection and failure, came up, I was an expert at defaulting to fix-it mode (otherwise known as cover-it-up mode, push-it-down mode, or run-like-hell-from-it mode). I'd turn to food, online shopping, or social media to try and escape the things that felt uncomfortable in an effort to change myself or, at the very least, change my state of mind.

But no matter how many brownies smeared in nut butter I ate, how many ankle boots I bought, or how many photos of perfectly poured lattes I double clicked, the yucky feeling remained. Often it was magnified thanks to the aforementioned "fixing" techniques. Scrolling through Instagram and seeing some fashion blogger's photo shoot didn't make me feel any better about a tight pair of jeans. Eating an entire tray of brownies didn't make me feel any more comfortable, either.

Shocking!

I spent a lot of years thinking that by feeling uncomfortable, I was doing something wrong. I imagined that if I were skinnier (or had the perfect job, or traveled the world for a year), I'd never have to feel anything other than happy. I didn't think *the feeling* needed fixed. I thought *I* needed fixed for feeling it.

I've tried to remember when I started to believe that feeling something uncomfortable meant, "You need fixed!" rather than, "This needs felt." I don't have that perfect moment. What I do remember is the moment I decided to try something new.

At the time, I was working at the law firm and had a very challenging day at the office. One of the partners I worked with had said something very hurtful about me to another one of the partners, who then told me. I felt rejected. I felt like a failure. And I felt heartbroken. It was all of my least favorite feelings wrapped up in a package I did not want to open.

I left the office and headed home. When I got there, I realized Tim wasn't home from work yet. The most binge-triggering time of the day for me was the hour or so after work when I was feeling exhausted, often struggling with anxiety, and home alone. I went into the kitchen and started rummaging. I went through the cabinets hunting for something that would make me less of a rejected, heartbroken failure. *MISSION ACCOMPLISHED!* I found a bag of pretzels, some cookies, chocolate chips, and a jar of peanut butter. *NAILED IT!* Extra points because I was confident I could smash all these foods up and eat them together in some sort of sweet-salty combo.

As I took out a mixing bowl, I heard my coach's voice in my head. She gently said, "If you choose to feel it, you can handle it."

I decided in that moment that I would try. After all, those pretzels would still be there in a few minutes, right?

I left all the food on the counter, went up to my bedroom, took off my bra (trust me: it's so much easier to feel feelings when you can ditch the bra), and got under the covers. It was still light out but I didn't care. I let all the weight of my head sink into the pillow and I cried my eyes out. I cried so hard. I cried because I had been working so much. I cried because, even if I didn't want it to, what that partner thought about me mattered to me. I cried because I thought she was my mentor and it turned out she didn't care about me the way that I thought she had. I cried because I was really unhappy at my job and it pissed me off that I was letting something that made me so unhappy make me even MORE unhappy. I cried because it felt good to cry. I just felt it ALL. Once I got started feeling, it was like I entered the calm eye of the storm. It actually felt so quiet to be in the midst of so many feelings. I just let myself lay there, feeling and crying, for a long time.

The next thing I knew, Tim was waking me up. "Are you sick? Is everything OK?"

I guess somewhere between sobbing like a child and feeling all the feelings, I had fallen asleep.

My eyes were swollen and itchy from all the tears, but I was pleasantly surprised to find that my answer to Tim was, "Yes!! I'm OK!" Just like my coach had promised, I *was* able to handle it. I was suddenly free to feel uncomfortable feelings. The best part about feeling it? The release that came after.

Since then, I've tried to remember to do less fixing and more feeling.

So, on that Monday morning when all of my fixing flopped, I remembered this. I remembered to fix less and feel more.

I looked Osh in the eyes and said, "Sometimes we just feel sad and, hey! It's OK to feel sad." I gave him a hug, let him cry, and pretty soon he fell asleep. Like mother, like son.

Preach It, Cher!

"How you do one thing is how you do everything," a teacher once told me. I didn't get it until I got it. And then I really got it.

Billing hours as an attorney was such a weird concept. On one hand, it was highly annoying to have to track all of my time. On the other hand, when I had a day where I was ultra productive and filled every second with work, it gave me a pseudo-high. A sense of superhuman accomplishment.

I was having one of those superhuman days when I started to feel an annoying distraction. My chest was getting tight. I kept trying to ignore it because, as I mentioned, I was busy billing those hours. I wanted to keep riding the momentum and cranking out the work. I did not want to deal with whatever was happening in my chest. But my body seemed to have other plans, and the more I tried to ignore the feeling, the more intense it got. It squeezed my chest so tight that I found myself struggling to breathe.

I gripped my chest and wondered, *Is this a heart attack?! Aren't I too young to have a heart attack?!*

The wondering turned into a full-on frenzy.

Wait, how do I check for a heart attack?

117

Do I smell burnt toast?

No, that's not a heart attack, that's a stroke!

THINK, SIMI, THINK! WHAT IS HAPPENING TO MY BODY?!

My legs went numb, so I did the only thing you can do when your legs go numb: I hit the ground. I lay there under my desk, feeling the moments that I wasn't billing slowly slipping away, feeling my chest shrinking, feeling my heart racing, and feeling my face twitching.

Is this dying?

I began to take inventory of all the details of my life that day. After all, if it were to be my last day, I wanted to remember it all.

I tried to remember what underwear I had put on that morning. *Are they last-day-on-earth underwear? NO! THEY DEFINITELY ARE NOT LAST-DAY-ON-EARTH UNDERWEAR. I can't die in this boring pair of underwear!*

"I don't want to die in these very not special underwear. I don't want to die here. I don't even want to work here." I whispered, realizing the words I was saying as they were coming out of my mouth.

Tim tells me that I'm very loud. So, for point of reference, my whisper is probably closer to a normal person's "outside voice." My whisper was so loud that my assistant sitting outside of my office heard me talking to myself.

She came to my office door, gently knocking as she pushed it open.

"Simi? Everything OK in here?" she asked.

My feet and legs were sticking out from under my desk, but my head was hidden. "Everything's OK," I lied. "Just stretching my legs for a second."

Believable.

A few days later, I sat there on the crunchy paper in my doctor's office feeling that level of discomfort that only the crunchy doctor's office paper can make you feel. My doctor told me that I had neither experienced a heart attack nor a stroke. I also hadn't died (clearly). The diagnosis was a panic attack. According to her, some things needed to change. She said I could go on medication (which I did) to help, but that it wasn't a magic pill. I had to get clear on what I wanted in my life and make some changes to support my mental health, not just my physical body.

I later asked my family, "Can you believe *I* had a panic attack?" For the record, I wasn't *really* asking, but they didn't get that.

"Uhhh, yeah..." they all replied independently. Nobody was surprised. Turns out I was the only person who didn't realize how tightly I was wound.

WHO ASKED YOU?, I thought.

Have you ever had a conversation with someone who ignored most of what you said? Or dated someone who disregarded everything you told him or her you needed? Or worked your butt off giving your all to a project, only to have your boss gloss over your hard work ... or worse, tell you it totally sucked? That's what I imagine it was like for my heart and my body all those years. Telling me things. Asking for things. Working so hard for me. Just to be ignored, disregarded, and deemed not good enough.

I didn't have any trust with myself; I eroded it all trying to be perfect.

In her book, "Braving The Wilderness," Brené Brown explains the anatomy of trust. She shares Charles Feltman's definition of trust, which is "choosing to risk making something you value vulnerable to another person's actions."

Brown then breaks down the elements of trust with the acronym BRAVING:

BOUNDARIES
RELIABILITY
ACCOUNTABILITY
VAULT
INTEGRITY
NON-JUDGMENT
GENEROSITY

For years, I didn't do B, R, A, V, I, N, or G for myself. What was important to my body and to my heart wasn't safe with me. I ignored what I needed. I ignored what I liked. I made zero effort to ask or listen or even pretend to care. I judged myself. I went to everyone else to decide what I "should" do instead of checking in with myself on what I actually needed. I sought out what I believed would make me more likeable rather than focusing my energy on the things that mattered most to me. I disregarded boundaries in favor of saying "yes" to whatever I thought would make someone else happy. I told myself hurtful stories and lies.

Whatever's the opposite of BRAVING, that's what I was doing.

It's hard to have a healthy relationship with someone you don't trust.

When I decided to go to law school, I didn't question whether being an attorney was my calling or my passion. I didn't know myself. It felt easier to ask other people what I should do than to actually get curious about what would make me happy or fulfilled.

After years of having no clue what I actually liked, needed, or wanted to do, it felt really strange to acknowledge on one random afternoon at the office that I actually didn't want to do what I was doing.

HI. A LITTLE SOONER WOULD HAVE BEEN IDEAL.

I went to law school and I got a job at a law firm. Every day I looked around and saw people who were so fulfilled practicing law. They would light up when they talked about their work. They were inspiring and on fire! I was not.

And I felt like something was wrong with me because I didn't feel the way that they felt (or, at least that I perceived they felt).

It wasn't that I thought being an attorney was awful. I really respect the profession. I really *wanted* to love it. But I just didn't. And knowing that it wasn't what I was meant to do but still pushing myself so hard to do it created major internal friction.

But I pushed the feelings down and pushed forward. I thought, *If I can just do this perfectly — bill more hours, get my own clients, make partner — then maybe that will make me feel like they feel.*

For a long time, that was how I did everything. Because how you do one thing is how you do everything. I would feel the friction, think it meant something was wrong with me, fantasize about a day when I would be perfect enough that it would no longer feel friction-y (is that a word?), and try harder.

I guess the doctor was right. Some things really did need to change.

What I learned from that panic attack was that at least one thing had already changed. And that one thing was slowly changing everything else.

I can now see that one of the single most life-changing moments of my life was deciding that I was no longer going to make all my problems — all my worth, all my lovable-ness, all my identity, all my success, all my everything — about my body.

If some weird airbrushed ideal and made-up "goal weight" perfection was no longer required to know that I was OK, then I would no longer need to white-knuckle my relationship with food and exercise.

So I made the decision that my body would not longer dictate my worth. I decided that a specific number on the scale was no longer required to give myself permission to live my life.

It wasn't a one-time decision, and it didn't happen with a simple snap of my fingers.

At first, it was a million times a day. Minute by minute. I had to constantly remind myself what I actually valued, why this shift was important to me, and that I was safe to be myself. I had to remind myself that weight loss as a guarantor for love and acceptance was a total fantasy I had created (with the help of millions of dollars of advertising). I had to remind myself how hard it is to give up fantasies and practice self-compassion and grace.

I believed in Santa Claus until my fifth grade teacher said to the class "Well, since I know none of you believe in Santa Claus anymore ..."

WHAT?!

Talk about a traumatic end to a fantasy. I cried for days.

So you can imagine what it was like for me to give up my just-look-like-an-Olsen-twin-and-everything-will-be-OK fantasy I'd been entertaining.

Before I could learn to trust myself, I had to have a good cry. I had to mourn! To mourn the loss of hope that I would one day look like an Olsen twin. I had to mourn the loss of hope that came when I decided that weight loss was no longer my goal. I had to mourn the loss of everything I had done, thought about, read, and invested my time in for years in an attempt to make my body perfect. On a deeper level, I had to mourn the loss of my perceived purpose and who I had come to believe I was.

It's not just the awesome relationships that are heartbreaking to say "goodbye" to. Ending unhealthy, abusive relationships can be incredibly hard and sad, too. And this was the most powerful breakup of my life.

I was breaking up with who I believed I needed to be to start a relationship with who I truly was. Who I truly am.

For so long, my whole existence was focused on losing weight. Everything I read was to find a way to lose a few more pounds or "jumpstart" my metabolism, like it was some kind of car battery. My free time was spent writing plans and counting calories and documenting and re-documenting everything I'd eaten. My days were scheduled around workouts and rigid sleep schedules. All of my mental energy went toward trying to fix my body.

No wonder I didn't have the mental space to decide what I felt called to do in my life!

Giving up this focus felt disorienting.

I was lost, confused, and directionless. As the great Cher in "Clueless" so eloquently states, "I felt impotent and out of control, which I really, really hate."

PREACH IT, CHER!

Who was I if I didn't have weight loss?

I didn't know. But, I decided to trust that whoever I was, I was a person worth getting to know.

This meant that, over and over again, I had to release unnatural and unrealistic expectations for myself. The release really started with my food rules. One by one, I released my rigid food rules in exchange for learning to hear and trust in what I needed. And things started to shift. Slowly. Gradually. In a two steps forward one (sometimes three) step back kind of way.

When I would hear that voice inside me telling me what I "should" or "shouldn't" eat, I'd yell, *STOP!*

I think I mentioned that I'm not quiet, yes?

Then I'd shift my thinking from *Will this help me lose weight?* to *What is my body asking for? What do I truly need? What would feel good and supportive to my whole self?*

I tried to come from a place of nourishment rather than punishment.

At first, it was hard because there were a lot of shoulds and shouldn'ts. Many of them even conflicted. There were moments where I felt like I was losing my mind with so many voices telling me what to do.

But I kept trying to quiet them so I could hear myself. And over time it became easier to hear what I needed. It was like learning a new language. I also learned that a little curiosity goes a long way. I started to hear my body ask for food and I began to understand what would feel satisfying. Not only did I begin to trust my body to ask for what she needed, but she began to trust me to give her what she asked for.

We were definitely BRAVING!

And, because how you do one thing is how you do everything, I started to listen more in all areas of my life. Curiosity took the place of judgment. Nourishment rather than punishment began to feel normal. Soon, I not only listened to what I was hungry for on my plate — I heard what I was hungry for in my *life*.

That day, as I lay under my desk, the voice was loud and clear.

The more I listened, the more I heard.

The Nice Place in Between

When Tim and I first moved in together, we lived in a small one-bedroom apartment in Chicago. We moved in during my first-year law school finals, and to say I was stressed would've been a slight understatement (about the finals, not living with Tim). His parents came into the city to help Tim move the furniture from my studio apartment into our new one-bedroom apartment, both of which were in the same building but on different floors. While they were doing all of that heavy lifting, I was at the library drinking strong coffee and studying. They are serious gems.

That evening, I came home from a day at the library to a mostly unpacked apartment. Rather than being grateful, I was annoyed. He'd unpacked my bathroom items and put them in the wrong drawers. He'd unloaded the spices and put them in the wrong cabinets. He'd unwrapped pictures and hung them on the wrong walls.

HOW DARE HE TRY TO ORGANIZE MY, I MEAN, UH, OUR APARTMENT?!

With a fierce attitude, I started huffing and puffing around the apartment. On some level, I knew I was being irrational so I didn't technically want to say why I was annoyed, but on another level I

WAS ANNOYED, and I wanted him to know. Hence the huffing and puffing with no use of actual words.

I slammed some cabinets. I pressed my feet into the ground harder with every step. I sighed. Subtle.

"Everything OK, Sim?"

"Mmmmmhmmmmm." I curtly replied. I love words, so no real words is a sure sign that everything's not OK, OK?

"You seem upset about something. Did anything happen at school?"

"ONLY STUDYING FOR HOURS AND HOURS ONLY TO COME HOME AND FIND THE SPICES WHERE THE SPICES DON'T GO AND EVERYTHING ELSE WHERE EVERYTHING ELSE DOES NOT GO!" I exploded.

"Wait, what?" he said, looking very concerned and also confused. "You're upset about spices?"

"IT'S NOT ABOUT SPICES!"

Now he was very confused. "But I thought you just said something about spices?"

"IT'S ABOUT RESPECT!" I cried as I stormed into our bedroom and shut the door. I tried to slam it, but the carpet resisted. Once in the bedroom, I realized there was nothing for me to actually do. I left my laptop in my bag by the front door. We had no TV set up in our room. There were no books to be seen, and I must've left my phone on the counter. I just sat there on the bed.

WHAT TO DO, WHAT TO DO?

There was nothing to do but sit with my own thoughts and less-than-ideal behavior. I took a few deep breaths and began to see that I may have overreacted a bit. With every inhale and exhale, the error of my ways became more clear. I felt really badly about how I acted, but I wasn't ready to apologize. Eventually the boredom overtook me and I had no choice but to emerge from my pouty cave.

I walked into the family room to find Tim sitting on the couch.

"Did you get bored in there?" he asked.

He knows me so well.

I apologized to him and I really meant it. He didn't deserve to be treated that way, and I made sure he knew that I understood that. We talked about what was really going on and I fessed up to the fact that I have a very specific way that I like things, which happened to be in contradiction to the way that he had organized things.

"Everything doesn't have to be so black and white, you know. Things don't have to be your way or a total disaster. There is a really nice place in between."

He was so right. It was a simple truth, but simple isn't always easy for me.

Black-and-white thinking was something I struggled with a lot. I was someone who lived in extremes. Everything went according to my plan, or everything went to hell. It was all or it was nothing, all the time.

I was all or nothing with food.

I was all or nothing with exercise.

I was all or nothing with spice cabinet organization.

I was either drinking 10 cups of coffee a day or declaring that I was off coffee for good. I was either eating exclusively vegetables all day or pouring dish soap over raw cookie dough in the trashcan because it felt like the only thing that would make me stop eating it. I was either running and sweating for hours or lying in a dark room watching Netflix until the screen asked me, "Are you still watching?" *Yes, I am still watching. But thanks for reminding me that I've been watching "Fuller House" for the last three hours.*

There was no in between. I couldn't have one cup of coffee and see how I felt. I couldn't eat some veggies and some cookies on the same day. I couldn't go for a leisurely walk and let myself enjoy it. I couldn't watch a few episodes of a show without finishing all 10 seasons. I was missing all of those opportunities to experience the "nice place in between."

To be honest, when Tim first mentioned the "nice place in between," I didn't think that place was for me. Extremes came naturally to me. Being in the middle did not. I thought to myself, *He can say that because he's an in between person and I am an extreme person. This is just who we are.*

Over time I realized that I didn't want to be the kind of person who locked herself in the bedroom for 30 minutes every time the spices were out of place. I didn't want to have to eat an entire tray of cookies or no cookies at all. I didn't want to feel like a heart-pumping hour-long exercise session was the only thing that could "count" (whatever "count" even means).

I realized that I had a choice to live life in those extremes, or discover what the in between could look like for me. I had to learn how to practice being in the nice place in between. And man oh man, did it take practice.

But these days, most of my life is the in between.

Most days I eat vegetables and cookies. I honestly can't remember the last time I got super sweaty working out. I can definitely remember the last time I took a walk, because it happens almost every day. I definitely can't remember the last time I "gave up" coffee.

After having Osh, I was drinking a lot of coffee. I love the taste and those sleepless newborn nights made it that much sweeter in the morning. But after a few months of throwing back multiple cups a day, I could feel that it was a bit too much for my body. I was getting jittery, feeling anxious, and my stomach was hurting a bit. The all-or-nothing part of me would have declared, *No more coffee!* But I've learned to practice the next step that comes after that first urge to go to the extreme. I've learned to ask myself, *What would feel more gentle to try first? What would it look like to find the nice place in between here?* Rather than giving up coffee completely, I just enjoyed that first morning cup and starting sipping tea most afternoons.

I thought, *OH MY! This is growth! One cup of coffee and some tea! How far I've come.* I've learned that if I celebrate the little moments, like not swearing off coffee for an eternity, then I have way more things in life to celebrate. And who doesn't like to celebrate?

Most mornings, I take a walk with my family to get a morning cup of coffee that I didn't swear off. It's a daily reminder of how nice it is, that place in between.

SHOWING UP / NAILING IT 23% OF THE TIME

That's a Lot of Pressure
for a Pair of Pants

I'm no good at following recipes. Well, I actually have no clue how "good" I am at it. I might be excellent at snow shoeing, karate, or driving boats but WHO KNOWS because I've never tried. It's the same with recipes. I just can't bring myself to try.

Instead, I like to get into the kitchen, throw a bunch of stuff into a bowl, pop said stuff into the oven, and hope for the best. I would say this works out about 23% of the time. And by works out, I mean produces something edible. And one fine Sunday just happened to be in that 23%.

VICTORY!

I made a successful banana bread loaf, sans measuring or recipe. I was feeling just like Martha Stewart (but I bet she has to measure). The bread looked so pretty that I got distracted and accidentally knocked over a big stack of glasses. The glasses then created a domino effect, knocking over another stack.

Don't panic. None got in the bread. *PRAISE THE LORD.*

Despite the fact that the loaf was spared from a glass shard massacre, I instantaneously felt myself getting upset.

Wait wait wait wait, you have a choice here, remember? I heard the less pissed voice inside of me saying.

I do? I asked myself, a bit confused because I felt pretty angry. And when I feel angry, I also usually feel like it's the only option.

PAUSE AND CHOOSE, my less pissed voice calmly responded.

This is what personal growth looks like, people: entire conversations inside your own head with different versions of yourself. WHO DOESN'T WANT THIS?!

I paused, *Apparently, I have a choice here* (sometimes I like to get sassy with myself). Then I asked, *What do I want to make this mean?*

I could make it mean that *nothing* ever works out perfectly and I *always* mess something up. The words "never" and "always" are pretty good indicators that I'm taking things in an unnecessary direction. Or, I could make it mean that a glass broke and it really is no big deal. I could let it mean something or nothing.

The most valuable thing I've learned as I've worked on my relationship with myself the past six years hasn't been how to eat intuitively or have a normal relationship with food or not exercise 10,000 hours in a day. It's been how to pause and simply ask myself:

What am I making this mean, about me, my value, my identity, my worth?

Is that the kind of power I want to give this?

In the past, I was so reactive that I didn't even realize this choice was available to me. It's so disempowering to feel like you have no choice. For me, no choice typically looked like this:

- I'd try on a dress that fit the previous summer to discover that it was a little snugger than I remembered. Without realizing I had a choice, I'd make this mean that I was doing something wrong, that I was lazy, that I had no willpower, that I needed to go on a diet, that I was less attractive, that I was less lovable, that I was gross, and that I MUST lose weight as quickly as possible.
- I'd try on a pair of jeans that fit last winter to discover that they fit a little looser than I remembered. Without realizing I had a choice, I'd make this mean that I'd done something right! I had permission to feel good about myself for a few moments before becoming scared that it wouldn't last.
- I'd get a compliment from someone saying that I looked thin. Without realizing I had a choice, I'd make that statement mean that I was more attractive, that I was more lovable, and that I must truly belong.
- I'd have an interaction with that same person two weeks later and she wouldn't make any comment on my physical appearance. Without realizing I had a choice, I'd make this mean that I must've gained weight, I wasn't as pretty, I wasn't as special, and I wasn't as loved.
- I'd eat a big meal and feel really full. Without realizing I had a choice, I'd make it mean that I couldn't be trusted around food and needed to measure out every single bite to avoid making the same mistake again.
- I'd notice that someone who I admired unfollowed me on Instagram. Without realizing I had a choice, I'd make this mean that I must've posted something upsetting, that I was annoying, that I'd made someone mad, and that I definitely did something wrong.
- I'd break a glass. Without realizing I had a choice, I'd make it mean that *nothing* ever worked out perfectly and I *always* messed something up. I'd also get really nasty with Tim for napping in the other room while I was in there smashing

glasses because maybe if he'd been in the kitchen it wouldn't have happened and HEY IT MUST BE NICE TO NAP.

I would've let each one of these make or break my day. Let's be honest, sometimes I let them ruin way more than that. I allowed these experiences to dictate my worth, my value, and my identity. That's a lot of pressure for a pair of pants.

Everything changed when I started to ask myself, *What am I making this mean and is that really what I want to make it mean?* I no longer had to be the reactive version of myself if I didn't want to be. Suddenly, a pair of pants feeling tight could mean that I needed to pick a different, more comfortable pair of pants for that day. Someone not complimenting me or unfollowing me didn't have to mean anything about how loved I am. A broken glass just meant I needed to get a broom (although a friend told me that in Latvia they have a saying that a glass breaks for luck, so maybe let's go with that).

Tim told me many times during what I will refer to as my Always And Never Freak-Outs that, "These things don't have to make you so upset if you don't want to let them." And, like most things my husband says to me, I brushed it off, telling him, "THIS IS WHO I AM!" Then, when somebody else told me the exact same thing, I would proclaim, "THIS IS A GENIUS IDEA. WHY HAS NOBODY EVER TOLD ME THIS BEFORE?!"

When I told Tim about my genius realization, he just looked at me, shook his head, and smiled. Because a lot of marriage is telling your partner what she needs to hear, and then waiting for someone else to tell her the same thing so that she can finally get it.

It's So Nice to Have College Simi Back

I recently heard an NPR story about the power of sharing food. In "Why Eating The Same Food Increases People's Trust and Cooperation," Shankar Vendantam explores the science behind breaking bread and why sitting down together to share a meal increases trust and helps people feel closer.

In the story, Ayelet Fishbach shares that "food really connects people. Food is about bringing something into the body. And to eat the same food suggests that we are both willing to bring the same thing into our bodies. People just feel closer to people who are eating the same food as they do. And then trust, cooperation, these are just consequences of feeling close to someone."

The story hit me so hard. Even though the story wasn't about dieting, it reminded me so much of my disordered dieting days. When I was trying to manipulate my body with food restriction, I felt so isolated. I never felt connected to the people around me and even the thought of sharing food with others created a deep anxiety. I didn't enjoy family dinners, birthday celebrations, or girls' nights.

When you only let yourself eat a small number of calories and limited types of food, it's hard to let even a tiny bite of that go. Restriction breeds scarcity and scarcity breeds possessiveness. It did for me, at least. If I could only eat a few hundred calories at a meal, I wasn't going to let a spoonfull of any of those calories leave my plate.

It wasn't just my perfectly portioned meals that I couldn't share. I couldn't share my "cheat" food either. I rarely ate foods that weren't part of my plan, so whenever I did, it felt like my only chance. If I "let myself" (which actually felt more like "giving up," "giving in," and "failing" all at once) eat some pizza or birthday cake or whatever, I had to promise myself that it would be the last time I ever ate that food again. That was the only way I would be safe to take that first bite: if I promised it was the last time.

If you're going to eat that pizza, it has to be just this once. After tonight, it's time to be good again. It's time to eat clean again tomorrow. You'll reset your body starting tomorrow. And then, you'll eat that way forever.

Since that pizza was my last pizza ever, I was obviously going to eat all of it and more. So, *No … I don't want to split a pizza.* And, *No … you can't have a bite. CAN'T YOU SEE THIS IS MY LAST HOORAH?! HOW CAN YOU TAKE A BITE OF MY LAST HOORAH PIZZA?!*

I was the victim here! *Are you really going to steal pizza from a victim?*

I didn't say this out loud, but rather with dagger eyes.

I would eat ALL the pizza, followed by anything else I didn't normally let myself eat that I could get my hands on, since the day was already ruined. Then, with a belly full of aches and a mind full of really mean thoughts about myself, I would get online to order my juice cleanse for later that week. I would cancel all my plans for those cleanse days, so that nothing could get in my way. Because the rest of my life started tomorrow! And being with people around food just seemed to get in the way of my success.

Mealtime made me feel isolated. I preferred to eat completely alone, because then I could prepare my food in the most measurable and controlled way. I would come up with excuses about why I couldn't meet friends for dinner. If I did go out, I would order with so many substitutions that when my food arrived, I felt alone. Other people would point to something delicious on the menu to enjoy together. Meanwhile, I would take something like lasagna and deconstruct it to the point that it would arrive as mushrooms and spinach on a plate.

"Yum! Mushrooms and spinach," I would say with a smile, blaming my order on my Celiac disease.

The people who loved me would tell me that they felt so badly that I had to order such boring things.

"I know, I know," I would say. "I wish I could eat something more fun! Being gluten-free is such a bummer sometimes, but this is just how it is when I go to restaurants! I promise I get to enjoy way more fun stuff at home, though, so don't feel badly for me."

Part of that was true. I really did wish I could eat something more fun. A heart cannot live on spinach and mushrooms alone, and mine was starving! But, the parts where I lied made me feel even more isolated than my plate of greens.

When someone would offer me a bite of her food, I would try to do the math. *What was that cooked in? Which ingredients are in there? How many calories are in there? ... 20 plus 120 plus, AH I CAN'T BE SURE!* If I didn't know exactly what was in a bite of something, it just wasn't worth it. I didn't want a single bite of food that wasn't part of my plan, which was different week to week as I tried to refine my method. If any of it touched my lips, then I would be tainted. The day would be ruined. And I would have to start all over again the next day.

I couldn't tell people how I was feeling because I knew they wouldn't understand. Other people could eat these foods and be OK. Other people's bodies weren't as sensitive as mine. Their metabolisms weren't as slow as mine. Their systems must function better.

I was different, I thought.

So I kept it to myself. My thoughts, my feelings, and my food.

When Tim would try to cook for me, I would freak out. I would print him specific recipes. I would swarm around him in the kitchen like a mosquito to make sure he measured perfectly. I didn't want him taking any liberties and accidentally messing up my hard work.

Exasperated, Tim would ask me, "Do you remember when we were first dating and you used to let me cook for you all the time?"

I did. I remembered going to his house one night in college and watching him make me fajitas. He cooked the chicken and the peppers in so much butter it would have made the creator of Bulletproof coffee uncomfortable. We talked while he sautéed and then we made a huge plate of fajitas and ate them together on his futon. It was awesome and dang, does that much butter taste good!

"Do you think you'll ever let me do that again?"

At the time, I wanted to let him. I just didn't ever think I could.

Thankfully, we have the power to surprise ourselves.

Over the course of a few years, I slowly learned to let go of the behaviors I had adopted to feel in control. I learned that my worth was not tied to how "clean" I ate. I just chose to believe that. Which meant it was something I could choose to un-believe, too.

Slowly, I let go of the calorie counting and the long list of foods I was and wasn't allowed to eat. I stopped using Celiac disease as an excuse for my disordered behaviors and I let go of the need to know exactly what was in every bite of food. I let go of the lie that I would never eat pizza again. I let go of the lie that I was a better person if I didn't.

I let go and I let go and I let go. And, the more I let go, the more I could let other people in.

And then, for the first time since college, I let Tim make me dinner.

He made tacos and I have no clue what he put into them. I didn't find the recipe and I wasn't in the kitchen when he prepared them. I laid on the couch reading a book, instead. When they were ready, he poured me a glass of wine and we sat at the table. He put the food on my plate and I took a bite. It was so good. At the end of the meal, he brought out some gluten-free cookie concoction with ice cream for us to share. And we did. I don't know how many bites of it I ate. I don't know what was in it. But, if I had to, I would guess a whole lot of sugar and butter.

When we finished, I didn't rush to clean up all of the dishes and neither did he. The kitchen didn't need to be perfect, and neither did I. So we sat and kept talking. We poured another glass of wine. Tim looked up from his glass and gave me the best compliment I could have received. "It's so nice to have college Simi back."

I thought so, too.

Who Wears Short Shorts?

I've already shared a bit of my sordid history with shorts. Years, nay decades, after that uniform-chaffing incident, I could still barely even think about a pair of shorts without feeling my inner thighs get a little fiery.

NEVER FORGET, they reminded me.

I learned to hate shorts. Well, first I learned to hate my thighs and *then* I learned to hate shorts. After years of body image work and self-acceptance, after being cool with my thighs and not wanting to change them, I still didn't wear shorts.

I can't find any shorts that fit me correctly!

Shorts are ugly!

I prefer dresses!

GIRLS ARE WEARING WHAT THESE DAYS? IS THAT A SHREDDED DENIM THONG?

These were all the ways I explained why I never wore shorts. *It's not a body image thing, shorts are just stupid.*

According to Gloria Steinem, "We teach what we need to learn."

I see SO MANY WOMEN waiting until they lose those 10, 20, or 30 pounds, fit into a smaller size, or can finally master "perfection" to allow themselves to do the things they really want to do. Buy clothes that fit them, take a dream trip, start a family, leave a job they hate to pursue a passion. I coach these women to treat themselves as if they already are enough to say "yes" to these things. To connect with what they deeply desire to say "yes" to, I often have them work through a simple but super effective journaling exercise:

If there was NOTHING about me to fix…

I would/could…

Do/say/try/be/feel/wear…

_____!

I would tell those amazing women, "You have permission to wear the shorts you haven't let yourself wear *right now*! You deserve to feel comfortable this summer! You're worthy of it!"

They were wearing the shorts. They were liberating themselves from negative stories that had been holding them back! They were liberating their legs!

Meanwhile, I was wearing a dress.

I didn't realize this until I had Osh and needed to breastfeed during the hot summer months. Do you know what is 100% not breastfeeding-friendly? Every single dress in my closet. Literally, every single one. So, instead, I wore jeans. Jeans and a T-shirt were very breastfeeding-friendly. Unfortunately, jeans are not 95-degree summer-day friendly and my lower half was sweating profusely.

I would stand in my closet every single morning thinking, *Hmmmm these dresses won't work but those pants are so hot. What to do what to do.*

I had zero ideas about what I could do. Until a lovely coaching client told me she was having the same conundrum and without missing a beat I asked, "What about shorts?"

"Oh I don't wear shorts. My thighs are too big for shorts."

We went through the entire exercise above and ended our session with her ordering three pairs of shorts to wear the rest of that summer. Meanwhile, I was sitting with swamp ass.

If shorts were comfortable, nursing-friendly, and kept me from resting in my own puddle of sweat for hours each day, *WHAT IS THE REALLY GOOD REASON WHY I'M NOT WEARING THEM?*

My thighs are too big for shorts, I answered.

I believed my thighs were good enough for everything except shorts. I let myself sit with this belief for a while. I practiced some compassion with myself for carrying around this limiting belief for so long without even realizing it. I recognized that I'd unintentionally and subconsciously acted on something that I actually didn't really even believe anymore. I didn't need to believe it anymore.

So, I bought myself some shorts.

As Sarah Silverman says, "Mother Teresa didn't walk around complaining about her thighs – she had shit to do."

I'm not Mother Teresa, but I think this applies to all of us. So, I bought some shorts and got some shit done wearing them.

Would you believe it? I love shorts.

I'm Falling Behind According to Instagram

One minute I was hanging with my family, talking about what movie we wanted to watch after dinner, and the next thing I knew I was staring at Instagram.

BAM. How did that happen?

Without even realizing it, I had opened up the app and my thumb was doing a great job with a subconscious scroll sesh. Drooped over on the couch like the Hunchback of Notre Dame (read: the opposite of that power pose I saw on a TED talk once), I flipped through images, double-tapping pictures of s'more bars, unicorn quotes, succulent gardens, and family vacations. Innocent enough. I was loving life and everyone else's, too.

Smile and like.
Smile and like.
Smile and like.

And then I saw it. Something that didn't make me smile. Something I didn't like. I could feel my happy, double-clicking little heart sink all the way down into my stomach. A friend was going to be a guest on a huge podcast. A podcast I loved to listen to and *dreamed* of being on. I was so freaking happy for her. I was also the opposite of freaking happy for myself. I wanted to cry.

I'm falling behind according to Instagram!
I'm irrelevant.
My business is going under.
I don't work hard enough.
I'll never be on that podcast. I'm not on her level.
I'm never going to make it in this world!

Not only did the thoughts make me want to cry, but the thought of having the thoughts made me want to cry, too. I didn't want to let this bother me! But it did. I felt icky and stuck. I felt jealous. Jealousy feels like my heart is rotting. I am not a fan of a rotting heart.

I reminded myself, *Sim … you're human. It's normal to have these feelings. The work never stops.*

I caught myself in the lies. That what I have, what I'm doing, and who I am isn't enough; that someone else's success means anything about me, especially that I'm failing or falling short; and that our journeys (or businesses or bodies or families or lives) are meant to look the same.

I let those lies go and breathed in a little truth: *they are, it doesn't, and they aren't.*

PHEW.

Years ago, this would have turned into a month-long detox (because surely my "shortcomings" were being fueled by toxins). I would project my fear of not being good enough all over my body. This time, it was a few-minute spiral before coming back to reality.

I lifted my eyes from my phone and looked around.

For a few moments, I'd forgotten it was all there right in front of me. I saw my sweet family. I saw our cozy home. I saw notes on the kitchen table from client sessions earlier in the day that I had loved. I saw cookie crumbs on that table, too, from dessert shared with the people I love most. I saw MY life.

You know when you give two kids gifts at the same time and one decides that the gift you gave him is a piece of crap and he wants the other gift instead?

"But, I want that one!" he whines.

I felt like I had a lot in common with that kid.

That podcast was a gift handpicked for my friend. All around me were the gifts handpicked for me.

"I want these ones … they are perfect for me," I whispered.

"What are you talking about?" Tim said.

Not awkward at all.

Don't Forget the Coconut Water

I have a strong propensity to plan. It's always felt like part of my DNA.

When I was a kid, I'd plan out these elaborate games for my sister and I to play. I loved pretending like we were in an orphanage and she was very sick. Lucky her. It was the mid 1700s and I ran the orphanage. I knew in my orphanage-running wisdom that this child, my dearest sister, was ill and needed rest. I also knew that she needed a strict pill regimen to cure her illness, which was probably typhus given the year we were "living in."

I would make my sister lay on her back for hours while I made my rounds. Each hour, on the hour, I would place a single pink chalky candy (ahem, *pill*) on her tongue for healing.

In a turn of events that nobody could have seen coming, she'd tire of playing this game, ultimately escaping the institution (our living room) to go play with the neighbors' kids. I was left heartbroken, with only my fake pills to keep me company. *Why couldn't she just lie down there a little longer?!*, I wondered. For a control freak, messed up plans feel like loneliness, disappointment, and failure. *If she had just stayed there a bit longer, I wouldn't have to feel this way.* See, this is really about my sister's inability to play sick and helpless for more than three hours, not my inability to relax.

My urge to plan didn't stay in the 1700s with typhus. Neither did the subsequent feelings of loneliness, disappointment, and failure when things didn't go to plan. And they rarely did.

When we found out we were pregnant, evidently it was time to plan.

FINALLY! The sport I've been training for my whole life!

Everyone wanted to know about our birth plan. Was I getting an epidural? Going all-natural? Perhaps a deep water ocean birth? A small part of me was still hoping the baby was coming via stork delivery but "by large bird" didn't seem to be an appropriate answer. So, I did what every people-pleasing control freak does: I asked my friends before crafting a highly detailed birth plan.

After talking to some of my friends, it seemed that many had gone the "all-natural" route, which apparently meant no epidural. Every one of them spoke about their experiences very positively. That was all I needed to hear! "No epidural for me," I said. I, too, would go all-natural. Like in middle school when everyone, including Alex Mack, got bangs. "Bangs for me, too" I said. *Bangs look good on everyone, right?* (Wrong.)

The first order of business was to connect with an amazing doula who came highly recommended by a dear friend. Tim and I met her over very large iced teas at Starbucks (caffeine-free for me, nobody panic). We both instantly knew that she was the person we wanted to have in the hospital room with us. It was as if we were already a team. She was so calm, reassuring, and kind. She prayed with us. She encouraged us. She asked us great questions like, "What is your ideal birth scenario?"

Tim responded, "Safe Sim and safe baby."

I responded, "All-natural, baby." I thought I was funny. Like most of my jokes, it landed flat.

"Why is this natural birth the ideal scenario for you?"

I told our doula that I really wanted to feel connected to my body, to our baby, and to God during labor. I shared with her that I had spent many years working on my relationship with my body and food, and felt really connected to myself. After talking with friends who had given birth the all-natural way, it felt really right.

She helped me unpack this, while being incredibly supportive of my wishes. After talking through it a bit more, it became clear to me that an unmedicated birth wasn't necessarily the most important thing to me. Feeling connected was.

She wanted me to have an incredibly fulfilling labor experience. I wanted that, too. She advised that we make a wish list rather than a game plan. She explained that she had seen many women fixate on a specific plan and then feel discouraged and disheartened when something didn't go according to that plan.

"I know a thing or two about that," I told her.

Rather than writing out a strict plan that would define birth success, our doula guided me through a process to create my wish list. This wish list let me connect with my ideal scenario, map out what I would need to feel prepared for that scenario, and also release any expectations. The wish list allowed me to go into labor feeling prepared and open — rather than trying to plan something that was ultimately out of my control, only to experience loneliness, disappointment, and failure.

I left our meeting feeling so excited.

Months later, my due date came and went. I was still very much pregnant and my hospital bag had been packed for weeks.

On Sunday, September 4, I woke up around 5:45 AM with a serious stomachache. I was also pissed because, like I mentioned, I was still pregnant. I had never been late to anything in my life, so I had to wonder, *Is this kid even mine?* My insides were churning and I felt like I needed to go to the bathroom, but couldn't. I got back into bed feeling crappy. Soon, the stomach churning turned into cramps that traveled all the way around my back. *IS THIS LABOR?!*, I hoped with excitement.

I woke up Tim to tell him and make him join me for a walk. I wanted to do whatever I could to move labor along because I was ready to have this baby yesterday.

As we walked around our neighborhood, I could feel the contractions getting more intense. But they were nothing that I couldn't walk through. When I finally plopped down on the couch, I reminded Tim that we should probably time the contractions. They felt long, more intense, and closer together. The midwife group had told us that we would know it was time to go to the hospital when I was having contractions every five minutes, each for a full minute, for at least an hour. So, we decided to check in. Tim opened the app and we started tracking them. It didn't take us long to discover that they were lasting about 75 seconds each and coming every two minutes. Tim proposed we call our doula.

She came over immediately, and at this point I could hardly see straight. I felt like I was wearing blinders, and was totally unable to make eye contact. My legs were shaking. She said it looked like we were getting close to transition, so we headed to the hospital. I was struggling, but also so excited. We grabbed all the bags, headed to the car, and drove to the hospital. With the help of Tim, I was able to walk to check-in at Labor and Delivery.

Check-in is the place where someone asks you 40 million questions before you're allowed to have a baby. Some examples: "Can you confirm your birthdate and address?" "How do you spell your last name again?" and "What was the name of your first pet cat?" I was doubled over trying not to pass out. Her name was Pussywillow, for the record.

After what felt like an incredibly long interview process (I passed!), they admitted me and I got into a gown. One of the wonderful midwives came in to check on me.

"Are we having a baby tonight?" she asked.

"Yes!" I told her excitedly.

And then the excitement ended. To all of our surprise, I was only dilated to three centimeters. Forget the contractions. This news punched me in the gut! This news felt INSANE to me because I had basically been three centimeters at my appointment a few days before. I thought the baby was ready to come out of my body! She had done a manual check, so I asked, "Is there any chance you have MUCH smaller fingers than the midwife who checked me a few days ago?"

No. She had normal fingers.

"Am I about to give birth to a MUCH smaller baby than normal?"

No, again. We were having a normal sized baby.

The midwife recommended I put my clothes back on and go walk for an hour. I thought she was joking at first. She wasn't. So to the parking garage stairs we went! I walked the hell out of those stairs. I was lunging sideways. I was sweating like never before. Tim was complaining about the exercise the entire time. I was trying not to kill him with my side eye.

After about an hour of listening to my husband talk about how he "didn't sign up for an exercise class," we headed back for a second check. I was only three-and-a-half centimeters dilated.

The midwife told me I should go home and for the first time that day, I cried. I'm the kind of person who knows what she wants. And I did not want to go home. I wanted to have a baby! She gave me a hug and told me I could come back anytime.

"How will I know when to come back?" I asked.

"Just trust your body. You'll know." She encouraged.

"But, my body told me to come this time. So, can I come back now?" I pleaded.

She hugged me again and told me it would all be OK. Then she sent me home. We drove home, and in between contractions I cried some more. This was not on my wish list.

When we got to the house it was all a bit confusing. My contractions were incredibly intense. We tried some different positions in the bedroom (less sexy than it sounds) and then Tim spoon-fed me gluten-free mac 'n' cheese in between contractions (more sexy than it sounds).

After the mac 'n' cheese, I got into the shower and the hot water sent me into next level intensity. I was on the floor of the tub because I could not longer stand and started to feel scared. I had zero desire to have the baby at home and I told Tim I thought the baby was coming out at any moment. So, exactly 40 minutes after we got home, we turned around and headed back to the hospital.

This time was different. I couldn't walk anymore. So, when I tried to get out of the car I had to lie down on the parking garage floor while our doula went to get us a wheelchair. Sanitary, I'm sure. As I dusted up the floor with my hands and knees, Tim grabbed the bags from the car (again).

In between contractions, I yelled from down below, "Don't forget the coconut water!"

I might've been giving birth in a garage but damn if I was going to be dehydrated!

Once in the wheelchair (followed by Tim and enough coconut water to make Costco blush), we started the journey back to Labor and Delivery. On the way, we passed a group of kids who looked like they were in high school. As our doula wheeled me next to them, I whispered into the crowd "Abstinence, kids. Abstinence." They looked terrified. Clearly, my job there was done.

Checking into Labor and Delivery the first time is annoying. But checking *back* into Labor and Delivery after you've already checked in once, had to go home, and are having contractions so intense that you don't even care about laying on a parking garage floor? This is its own form of torture. As soon as Tim helped me get back into the gown, my water broke.

At this point, I don't really know what was happening. I was only four centimeters dilated. I honestly thought that baby was ready to fly out of me like some scene in "Ally McBeal," but clearly that wasn't true. They monitored my contractions and confirmed that the intensity and length of contractions were mimicking transition, but the rest of my body wasn't catching up. After a few examinations they confirmed that our little guy was lying sideways and my body was over contracting to try to get him to move into place. It wasn't working.

I was barely coherent, shaking, and blacking out for periods of time. I couldn't physically stand any longer, but somehow sitting was even more intense. They moved me to my delivery room and I made my way to the floor, my new favorite place to hang. On my way down I said, "Get me that epidural. Now."

Have you ever met someone and known, with your whole heart, that you were meant to be together? You instantly imagine being 90 together and still head over heels for each other? It's like every fiber of your being is confirming that, "YES, this is the one"?

That is exactly how I felt about the epidural.

I knew it in my bones. Meant to be. My one.

DO IT NOW!

"I want the epidural. I am 100% sure I want the epidural. I have never wanted anything more in my life. Please right now epidural right now please thank you right now."

I had no idea when you say, "Get me the epidural now," that it didn't come right through the door. Forty-five minutes later, the anesthesiologist came into the room and allegedly stuck a big needle in my back, per my request. To be honest, I didn't feel a thing. She could have been back there making flower arrangements and I wouldn't have known the difference. Until it started to work. And, let me tell you, I was a new woman. I was transformed into Dick Van Dyke a la "Mary Poppins," if he had been numbed from the waist down. I was making best friends with my nurses. I was laughing and telling jokes. I was low key trying to make out with our anesthesiologist, who was now my favorite person in the world (Tim wasn't mad. She was his favorite person, too).

The midwife checked me one more time at 11 PM, and I was still right around four centimeters. They told me to try to rest up for pushing the next day and turned off the lights, since apparently this baby wasn't quite ready to come out and join us.

Tim and our doula fell right to sleep. I lay there, wide awake, listening to Alyosha's heartbeat on the monitor.

I've never stayed awake all night long. Not in college, not in law school, not ever: until the night of September 4. I was so full of excitement to meet Osh that I couldn't fall asleep. I prayed the whole night, cried tears of overwhelming joy, and talked to the little guy I would meet soon. The room was completely dark, except for the little bit of light creeping in underneath the door and the lights outside. The beep, beep, beep of his heart on the monitor was the only thing filling the peaceful silence.

Every so often, a nurse would come in and check on me. She would whisper, "So sorry to wake you …" And I would pop up and say, "Who me? Oh no, I'm not asleep. Just wide awake here waiting for this baby!" I'm sure it wasn't creepy at all.

I can't remember a time when I've had more energy in my life. I actually considered Googling, "Are epidurals just a crap load of caffeine?" But since I didn't have my phone with me, I added it to a mental list of things I would Google whenever I got my phone back (a list that also included, "How dirty are parking garage floors?" and, "How much coconut water is too much?").

When 6 AM rolled around, the midwife came in to check me again. After a full night of contractions, I was only dilated to six centimeters.

Six centimeters?!

I couldn't believe it. At this rate, I wondered if Osh would even be here by Christmas.

With this news, Tim went to grab coffee. Actually, coffee is an understatement. Tim came back to the room with eggs, bacon, sausage, and some kind of pastry. From the second we got to the hospital he was a bottomless pit: eating all the snacks I had packed (for myself) and now a full-blown lumberjack breakfast. Hell, he probably drank all the coconut water, too! Not three minutes after my water broke he was standing next to me eating beef jerky. *THIS IS NOT A MOVIE, PUT AWAY THE BUTTERED POPCORN.* His ability to eat was almost more miraculous than the "miracle of life" itself.

At 7 AM, a new midwife came in to check me. This time, I was at nine-and-a-half centimeters and, according to her, Osh was ready to come on out! Our doula took a few moments to pray with us and by 7:30 AM I was at 10 centimeters, and we were all set up to start pushing. The midwife set some expectations for me: Pushing could take two minutes or two hours.

Osh took his time. Teaching me patience from the beginning. Two minutes would become two hours, then three, then four. They were the four most perfect hours of my entire life. Minutes passed, but I didn't notice. Hours passed, and I didn't notice those either. Time felt like it didn't exist. Much of my epidural had worn off by that point, so I was able to push easily with my contractions. I felt so calm in my body. So peaceful and connected.

At the three-hour mark, they called a doctor in to see if we needed to do a C-section or use forceps to get the little goose out, but she looked me right in the eyes and said, "Nope, you've got this."

I pushed for another hour and in a simple moment he arrived. Nine months of waiting, four hours of pushing, and in a single second there he was. The connection I felt was more than anything I could have ever dreamed. More pure and nuanced than anything I can put into words. It felt natural.

My labor experience didn't include a single thing from my wish list. Nothing went according to "plan." In that moment, I was able to see what a pure blessing that could be.

When things don't need to be a certain way to be good, a lot more things get to be good.

You've Got Child-Birthing Hips

I had so many expectations about pregnancy. I also learned a lot of lessons from pregnancy. The first lesson I learned from pregnancy was to stop having so many damn expectations.

Before becoming pregnant, I had expected to GLOW. I was to be a florescent goddess.

I envisioned myself like Demi Moore on the cover of Vanity Fair, but even dewier. I did not think these were unrealistic expectations, as most of the women I knew (including my mama) had shared with me how magical pregnancy was for them. I was so ready to step into this magical, ultra-feminine version of myself.

PREPARE THE NUDE PHOTO SHOOT, I thought when I saw that positive pregnancy test.

Important question for you: what's the opposite of glowing? Right around week six of my pregnancy, I started to do *that*. And I didn't stop until week 40 and two days (which was when Osh was born). I spent the vast majority of my pregnancy with my head in the toilet or in a plastic bag trying to get to the toilet. Standing up made me vom. Lying down made me vom. Smells made me vom. Breathing made me vom. The only thing that didn't seem to make me vom was chicken pad thai.

THANK YOU LORD FOR THE GLORIOUS GIFT OF
CHICKEN PAD THAI, which I doubt I'll ever be able to eat
again after eating it every day for approximately 34 weeks. I think
I've consumed enough to constitute "a lifetime supply."

When I got pregnant, my struggles with food, exercise obsession,
and hating my body were years in the past. I was in a really good
place and, in addition to glowing, I also expected pregnancy to be
smooth sailing.

All of my struggles are in the past! I'll love being pregnant.

Wrong.

Without a doubt, the nine months of pregnancy were some of the
most challenging I'd experienced yet. I spent many days lying on
my bathroom floor, getting sick, and praying for relief. I counted
down days, weeks, and months until I would feel better. Everyone
told me it would end soon: "12 weeks!" "No, 14 weeks!" "For sure
by 20 weeks!" they said. Those weeks came and went.

Maybe week 35 will be my lucky week? No? What about 37?

If one more person asked me, "Have you tried ginger for the nausea?"
Well, I can't make any promises about what would have happened.

I finally gave in and took daily doses of a "morning" sickness
medication. I'm putting that in quotes because the sickness was
not exclusive to the mornings. This helped me throw up about five
times a day rather than my previous 10 or 15. The medicine made
me verrrry tired. From what I understand, it was part sleep-aid, so I
was basically popping goodnight pills throughout the day.

At least once a day someone would say to me, "Your eyes look swollen! Must be pregnancy!"

NO, LADY, I CAN BARELY OPEN MY EYES BECAUSE I'M TAKING SOME KIND OF PSEUDO-SLEEPING AID TO KEEP ME FROM THROWING UP ON YOU RIGHT NOW.

That's what I wanted to say. But what I actually said was "Yep! Must be zee ol' pregnancy eyes!"

Right after, "You've got child-birthing hips! They are so wide that baby is just going to slide right out," hearing that I had swollen eyes or that my face "looked pregnant" were probably my second and third favorite compliments I received while with child. Not a one person told me I looked like Demi Moore on the cover of Vanity Fair.

This was so not the pregnancy I had expected.

Being sick all the time was hard, but what felt harder were the feelings that came with it. I felt incredibly isolated, trapped, and discouraged. I missed being the super energetic version of myself. I missed being able to enjoy food. I missed wanting to be social. I missed feeling at home in my body. I missed eating anything other than pad thai. I panicked about only eating pad thai. *Is this baby even getting anything he needs?!*, I worried, as I spooned another helping of rice noodles in my mouth.

At first, the distance between the expectations I had for pregnancy and my actual pregnancy was filled with a lot of guilt. I felt terribly that I wasn't a "better" pregnant woman: I didn't feel like the sexiest, womanliest version of myself, and I definitely wasn't glowing. Let's be real, I was an on-the-bathroom-floor-with-dried-rice-noodles-in-my-unwashed-hair shell of my former self. It sucked until one morning I had the urge to read a little daily devotional I had been gifted by my sister-in-law many years before (and had read many times over those years). I opened Sarah Young's "Jesus Calling," flipping to a random page while I prayed for God to speak to my nauseous heart.

Here's what I found waiting for me: "Sometimes My blessings come to you in mysterious ways: through pain and trouble. At such times you can know My goodness only through your trust in Me. Understanding will fail you, but trust will keep you close to Me."

I asked myself what I would need to do or believe to be able to trust in this challenge as a blessing.

I'd need to let myself off the hook. I'd need to accept that my experience was exactly what it needed to be. I'd need to see that this challenge was growing my character in ways that it needed to grow, was allowing me to feel things that I needed to feel, and showing me a perspective I needed to see so that I could best do the next thing I was meant to do.

I'd need to appreciate that I was a human having a human experience. I'd need to allow myself to struggle. I'd need to be honest with people about what I was feeling. I'd need to set some boundaries and re-prioritize. I'd need to believe that God could use a tough season in my life to make something beautiful.

That last one, well, I already knew it to be true.

I'd already seen God turn one of my biggest challenges into one of my greatest blessings. My relationship with food and my body, which was once a deep pain point in my life, had been transformed into one of the biggest places for love to flow in and out. God used my struggles with food as an opportunity for me to grow. He used it as a way for me to connect with other women. He used it as a way for me to find passion and purpose and creativity. There were many moments in my past when I prayed to be "cured" of those struggles. But, instead, God took me down the longer road to heal in deeper ways.

That longer road really gave my challenge the time to mature into a blessing.

I felt what I needed to feel. I grew in the ways I needed to grow. I saw things in new ways. I was a human having a human experience and it was all exactly what it needed to be. The fact that it was hard didn't mean I was failing. These were growing pains. In hindsight, I wouldn't have sped up a second of it. I needed every second of the challenge to make me who I am today.

Remembering all of that helped me realize that I was ready to allow life to unfold in its beautiful, messy, and unique ways. I was ready to feel the freedom in the release — the release of the guilt, the shame, and the expectations. I was ready to live in the moment with joy during the rest of my pregnancy.

To me, living in the moment with joy doesn't mean that everything is happy or fun. It doesn't mean that I don't have challenges. It doesn't mean that I don't ever feel sad. It definitely doesn't mean I have it all together. It's a constant willingness to be present with whatever it is that is happening in life and letting it be what it is. It means declaring, *This is my life and I'm not going anywhere!*

So I declared that to myself. Then I threw up again.

Maybe I would never be Demi Moore. But the world doesn't need another Demi Moore! She's doing a great job at it already.

What a weight lifted to have permission to be myself.

Simi Botic

I decided to be the real me, which meant it was time to get real with myself and the people who I trusted the most. Sometimes this meant that I could tell Tim that being so sick made me feel alone and I could really use a hug while I cried. Then I would let him hug me (but not too tight because of the previously mentioned nausea) even though I hadn't shaved in a dog's age and smelled like stale tamari sauce. Those hugs felt nice.

I gave myself permission to have as much fun as possible in bed. And by that I mean that I re-watched "Dawson's Creek" as many times as humanly possible. And when I couldn't watch a single episode more, I moved on to "Felicity" and "Gossip Girl." I rested more. I said "no" more. I let myself off the hook for a lot of the unnecessary things in life that I had been incorrectly calling "necessary" to make time for the most necessary things, like client sessions and writing the proposal for this book. And "Dawson's Creek." I let whatever I could do each day count as enough. I was gentle and tender with myself. I asked for help.

So many people told me it would be worth it and I would want to do it again. I'd have my head hanging in the toilet telling Tim, "One and done! I can't do this again!" I thought those other people had lost their minds. I told myself they didn't understand.

But at 40 weeks and two days, when I went from being sick and pregnant to not being pregnant any longer, I whispered to Tim, "Can we have 10 more?" It *was* so worth it.

A few hours after giving birth, our doula spoke the sweetest, most intentional words to us. She said, "Rather than praying for him to sleep through the night, pray to find joy in those midnight feedings." And I got it. It's not about the circumstances; it's about the perspective.

Nipple Pads Make Terrible Tissues

It was a really good morning so far. I had washed my hair (this is a bigger deal than it sounds) and put on mascara (this is the biggest deal). I had blocked the first half of my work day off to write this book, and decided to make it special by getting ready a little more than normal.

I was on my way to the car feeling pretty good about how put together I felt. As I unlocked the garage door, I saw my phone light up.

"Hey Mama! How are you?"

"Hi sweetie," she said. "I'm not doing too well."

I felt my legs go numb as my mom talked through her tears. My dad had been diagnosed with stage three melanoma about 18 months before. He had been receiving immunotherapy treatment, but something had shown up on his full-body scan that morning.

When I heard my mom's voice I knew that it wasn't good. It wasn't OK. My dad wasn't OK.

She explained to me that his cancer was back. It had spread to different areas of his body and was now stage four. She said a bunch of medical terms I didn't understand, which is the lifelong reality of having two parents in medicine and being the kind of person who would rather Google what Louis Hay has to say about medical conditions. I was paralyzed. I took deep breaths, told my mama that I loved her, and prayed to God for a miracle.

It doesn't matter how old I get. I carry the expectation of my parents being OK, having the answers, and reminding me (as many times as I need to hear) that there are no monsters under the bed. For me, seeing my mom or dad sad, sick, or scared is like discovering that monsters have taken up a permanent residence under my bed.

When we hung up the phone, I lost it. *NOBODY LIKES MONSTERS.* I was hysterical. I cried like a baby. A baby who was scared of monsters and had nobody there to look under the bed and say, "Nope, no monsters here!"

I cried and cried and cried some more.

Snot poured from my nose.

I let it all out. And then more came up, and I let that out, too.

There is something so comforting about the sound of your own sobs when you're sad. It's like the calming repetition of ocean waves.

As the sound of my own crying began to clear my mind, I had a little space to think. *Do I quit my life so we can spend every minute staring into each other's eyes?* I let myself feel it all. Confused. Suffocated. Sad. Hopeful. And a lot of things in between.

I felt like someone had punched me in the face. Then I caught a glimpse of myself in the rearview mirror. It looked like I had the two black eyes to prove it.

OF COURSE I CRY ON THE ONE DAY IN 2017 WHEN I WEAR MASCARA.

I rummaged through every compartment in my car trying to find a tissue. No luck. I looked in my bag with no luck again. I did, however, find a nursing nipple pad. *I'm basically lactating sadness from my face, so surely this will work.*

I unwrapped the oval-shaped pad and attempted to dab up my tears, snot, and smeared mascara.

If you ever wondered, nipple pads make terrible tissues.

Soggy pad in hand, I looked out the window. It was a pretty perfect summer day. My hair was clean. My legs were shaved. The irony of the way I felt on the inside compared to what was on the outside made me wonder if I was sitting in the middle of an Alanis Morissette song.

I sat in my car for a really long time, crying with incredible intensity. Getting exhausted. Sitting in silence. Thinking I would never have another tear to cry again only to surprise myself with more tears. This cycle repeated itself for quite some time before I realized it was time to go home.

Later that day, we went over to see my parents.

We drove the 25 minutes to their house in relative silence, with only the sounds of Osh snoring in the backseat. I couldn't help but think about my dad listening to me snore as a baby 31 years before. Nothing like cancer to make you feel nostalgic.

When I first walked in their front door, it was quiet. I could smell the Capri candle from Anthropologie perpetually burning in the kitchen. I don't know what I expected to see when I arrived, but to my pleasant surprise, what I saw was my dad. The same guy he had been the last time I saw him. And the time before that.

He got up from the barstool he always sits on, in the hospital scrubs he always wears (he might be retired from the practice of medicine, but he certainly isn't retired from the uniform), and came to give me a hug. At 6′5″, he has to bend in half to give me a hug.

This is one of my favorite things about my dad: the way he hugs. When my dad hugs you, he goes all in. He puts his head on your shoulder and lets you do the same to him. Even though he towers above most, he comes down to your level for a hug. He always squeezes tight and says, "Ooooh," as if he's been waiting to hug you all day and, *finally*, he gets to. I hug everyone. But my dad is different. He doesn't give his hugs away quite as freely. If you're lucky enough to be part of the select group of people he loves enough to hug, you're really in for a special treat.

When he let go I looked at him and said, "This is awful. This sucks!"

"I know sweetie. Everything is going to be OK."

I asked him how he felt and he replied with a laugh, "I feel like me! I'm still the same guy! Your same dad!"

And that was very true. He's the same guy. My dad.

I laughed. Laughing felt good.

When I crawled into bed with Tim that night, I started to feel my chest tighten and it got harder to breathe. It felt like I was trying to breathe the thickest, most humid air in the world. In a few moments, it felt like there was a thousand-pound weight sitting right on my chest.

I told Tim, "I'm scared about what might happen. I'm scared to think about how much I might have to miss my dad."

The anticipation of grief was so intense, pounding on my chest and demanding, "Feel me!"

It was so uncomfortable. So painful.

Over the next few weeks, I had more waves of that intense heaviness on my chest. I found myself reaching for my phone a little more than usual. I found myself obsessing over things that I didn't really care about — like that person who I never met but I randomly found out had unfollowed me on Instagram. And I couldn't stop trying to figure out WHY. *Why did she unfollow me? Did I do something wrong? What did I do to make her click that button?*

I didn't like the way obsessing about social media made me feel. The more I thought about it, the more friction I felt inside. It didn't feel good to be distracted from what I loved by something so insignificant. But I couldn't stop thinking about it. Trying to figure out what I "did wrong" was occupying way too much of my brain space and emotional energy. After bringing this asinine situation up to Tim for the 100th time, he told me "Sim, I don't think this is healthy. I think you should talk to your therapist."

I hadn't thought to call my therapist (maybe because I was too busy re-reading and re-thinking every one of my Instagram posts for the past month?), but now that he mentioned it, I couldn't schedule a session with her fast enough.

On the drive to her office, I always plan out exactly what I am going to say. I get really clear on what my issues are to save her time with her diagnosis. And then, every time I sit on her couch, I end up crying and she helps me realize what they really are. (Never my predetermined diagnosis.)

This time, she helped me see that obsessing over some stranger on Instagram was a convenient way to distract myself from everything going on with my dad. She reminded me of all the things I had reached for in the past to try to distract, numb out, and control.

MY THERAPIST IS A GENIUS AND SELF-MEDICATION IS SO SNEAKY.

She reminded me to be kind and compassionate with that part of myself that was still trying to go back to the old ways. To sit with that part of myself. And to let her know it was OK to feel whatever I needed to feel. Then, she helped me feel what I really needed to feel: the grief. She reminded me that we grieve how we love, and because I love hard, grieving was probably going to be hard, too. Then she reminded me that I can handle hard.

She was right.

"Show up for what this is. Don't miss this," she said.

I held onto those words for a few moments. I let myself cry.

The girl who wanted to miss the hard stuff, well, I'm not that girl anymore. I don't want to miss any of it. I'm choosing to show up, instead.

Acknowledgments

Writing this book has been one of the coolest, wildest, most challenging, and deeply fulfilling things I've ever experienced. I most definitely didn't (and couldn't) do it alone.

Since I'll ~~probably~~ never win an Oscar, I'm going to take this opportunity to pretend like I just did (because you know I've spent numerous hours of my life planning my Oscar speech like I've got nothing better to do with my time):

~~I'd like to start by thanking the Academy…~~

To each person reading this book, thank you for being here with me. It means more to me than you know. Thank you for allowing me to share my authentic self with you. I hope this book encourages you to share your authentic self, too.

To my family and dearest friends, thank you for loving me through every story in this book and so many more that are unwritten. Thank you for laughing with me and crying with me and smacking some sense into me when I need it the most. Thank you for loving me when I didn't love myself (and for teaching me how it's done). You're my whole world and I love you!

171

To my sweet Alyosha, I got the idea for this book when you were in my belly and I truly feel it was a gift from you. Knowing you is the greatest joy and inspiration of my life.

To my partner for eternity, Tim thank you for not thinking I'm crazy when I get an idea like, *I'm going to write a book!* Thank you for believing in me. Thank you for building a life with me that always includes making space for big dreams. I'll love you forever and ever, amen.

To my clients and the women who let me into your lives and trust me on your journeys, thank you! You're my *why*.

To my mentors and teachers, where would I be without you? I'm so happy I don't have to find out the answer to that question. THANK YOU for your guidance, love, honesty, and support.

To Brigette, my wonderful family, and amazing friends who stepped in when I frantically texted, "help!," thank you for spending such quality time with Osh while I wrote this book. He's so blessed to be loved by you and so am I. It takes a village! Knowing he was being loved and cared for by you guys made my time working on this project possible.

To the inspiring women who collaborated with me on this project (pinch me, because I can't believe I get to call you the best of friends): Jessica, thank you for being the most amazing editor, holding me accountable the whole way, and walking with me step by step through every word of this book. Katie, thank you for encouraging me to go to the Hay House Writer's Workshop and writing the beautiful Foreword that brought me tears of joy. Joslyn, thank you for working your artistic magic that I've admired since 5th grade and creating the illustrations that truly bring these stories to life. Allie, thank you for designing a forever home for my stories with a cover more wonderful than I ever could have imagined. Thank you all for your friendship. What an honor to collaborate with each one of you! I love you to the moon and back.

To the amazing Hay House and Balboa Press, thank you for seeing something in my proposal, investing in me, and bringing this book to the world. I am so grateful for you and I am humbled by this opportunity. It means the world to be part of your incredible community.

Printed in the United States
By Bookmasters